TANKMASTER

A practical guide to

BREEDING
YOUR FRESHWATER FISH

DEREK LAMBERT

INTERPET PUBLISHING

Author

Derek Lambert, a passionate fishkeeper for over 30 years, has bred hundreds of species of fish. He has travelled the world in search of new and rare species and is involved with several conservation projects. His fish room contains 100 aquariums housing a wide variety of fish. He is Editor of Aquarist and Pondkeeper magazine and is also involved with several television projects.

© 2001 Interpet Publishing,
Vincent Lane, Dorking, Surrey, RH4 3YX, England.
All rights reserved.
ISBN: 1-903098-03-3

Credits
Created and designed: Ideas into Print,
New Ash Green, Kent DA3 8JD, England.
Production management: Consortium, Poslingford,
Suffolk CO10 8RA, England.
Print production: Sino Publishing House Ltd., Hong Kong.
Printed and bound in Indonesia.

Below: A cute brood of baby bristlenose catfish. This is one species of fish that will often breed successfully in a community aquarium, with small fry just appearing one day.

Contents

Rams are good parents that defend their offspring courageously.

Introduction

Giving nature a helping hand

Many aquarists are put off breeding their fish because they think it is difficult or complicated. In fact, nothing can be further from the truth. In most aquariums the fish will be breeding off and on just about all the time! The trick is stopping the other fish eating any eggs or young and being able to rear the offspring.

Livebearers are where most people start, usually accidentally. A female guppy will drop fry in a community aquarium and, if they are spotted in time, the fishkeeper will grab a net and save the fry. Nothing difficult about that, and many people become hooked on the idea of breeding fish from this first experience.

Cichlids are another group that often introduce their owners to the joys of breeding fish. Many species will decide to breed in a community aquarium and will often tear up all the plants and cause general mayhem in the process. However, watching a pair of cichlids bringing up their family is enchanting, and many aquarists become gripped from that moment on.

Apart from the sheer pleasure of watching your fish breeding, there is another very important role this activity plays. While most fish are captive bred in fish farms around the world, a significant number of species are still collected in the wild. Cardinal tetras, discus and many catfish species are exported by the million from the Amazon Basin. Some decline in wild stocks has now been noted and concerns have been raised about certain species that have all but disappeared from the wild because of overfishing.

The more fish are bred by aquarists, the less pressure there will be on the wild stocks. So what starts as a pure hobby can actually have a significant effect on conservation issues. Indeed, thanks to aquarists a number of species still exist in captivity that have become extinct in the wild. *Skiffia francesae* (the golden sawfin goodeid) probably died out in the wild over two decades ago, yet they remain in aquarists tanks and have recently been returned to Mexico with a view to reintroduction to the wild. Likewise, cherry barbs are in serious decline in the wild (due to habitat destruction) but many millions of them grace aquariums around the world.

Many species of fish require certain water conditions if they are to breed successfully. Many characins, for example, need very soft acidic water if their eggs are to hatch successfully. Likewise, some killifish have problems if the water conditions are not correct for them; the eggs of the checkered pupfish *(Cualac tessellatus)*, for example, will hatch prematurely in soft water.

To check water quality, you will need pH and hardness testing kits. There are plenty of these available, including electronic versions that may seem very expensive but could, in the long term, save you money. If you need to alter the pH or hardness, it is important to do so slowly. Rapid fluctuations of either of these will stress fish and, in the case of pH, may kill them outright.

Softening water

In many areas, the tapwater will be too hard for the breeding of some of the more sensitive species. If this is the case, you will need to soften the water. There are

Water testing kits are an essential piece of equipment when breeding fish.

several ways of doing this; using a reverse osmosis (R.O.) system is particularly popular at the moment. However, these produce huge quantities of waste water and the usable water will be too pure for many fish to breed in. The solution is to dilute the R.O. water with tapwater until you obtain the correct hardness reading.

A cheap alternative to R.O. water is to collect rainwater from a clean roof and filter it through activated carbon. The disadvantage of rainwater is that it may contain all kinds of pollutants (particularly in industrialised areas) that can harm eggs, fry or even adult fish.

Hardening water

It is easier to harden water because it simply involves adding one of the many proprietary chemicals sold for Malawi cichlid aquarium setups. Alternatively, you can filter your water through coral sand, which will also harden it up.

Creating a peat substrate

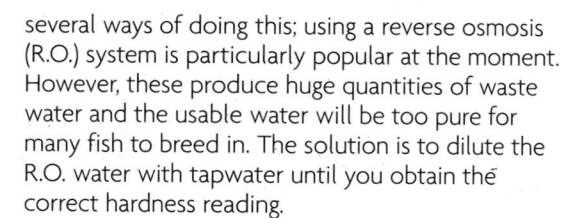

Left: Crumble a 5cm (2in)-thick layer of peat onto the water surface. Use either rainwater filtered through carbon or R.O. water mixed with tapwater to achieve the correct hardness.

Left: The peat will initially float on the surface and may take a week or so to sink to the bottom. Stirring it every day and squeezing pieces that are full of air helps to make it sink more quickly.

Above: The water is now acidified and contains many beneficial trace elements. You can siphon it into another container for use with those fish that require soft, acidic water or use the tank as it is for substrate spawners or characins that are sensitive to light.

Altering the pH

It is fair to say most aquarists confuse pH and hardness. While it is true that most hard water is alkaline and most soft water is acidic, there are exceptions. In any case, soft water out of the tap will generally not be anywhere near acidic enough for spawning tetras and other acid-loving fish.

One way to acidify water (i.e. to lower the pH from the neutral reading of 7) is to fill an aquarium with rainwater and then cover the surface with about 5cm (2in) of dry peat. After about a week, the peat becomes waterlogged and drifts down to the bottom, releasing chemicals that acidify the water and stain it brown. The resultant dark tea-coloured water looks identical to that found in the Rio Negro in the Amazon Basin and in other 'blackwater' areas.

Coral sand used as a substrate will push up both the hardness and pH levels and is probably the best way of raising the pH naturally. There are, of course, plenty of chemicals available from your local aquarium dealer and you can use these to raise or lower the pH as needed. Make sure you follow the directions carefully and never change the pH rapidly.

Filters in breeding tanks

Filters are available in all shapes and sizes, but not all are suitable for a breeding tank. Those that create strong water currents can suck in small fry or disturb bubblenests or other spawning sites. In general, it is best not to include a filter initially. However, if the adults are going to occupy the aquarium for long periods (many cichlids spawn in permanent setups) filtration will be needed. In most cases, a simple bubble-up sponge filter is the best choice. This is gentle enough not to be a threat to the fry, but will provide sufficient filtration for one pair of fish in a breeding tank.

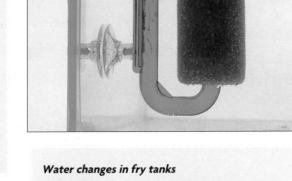

Right: Bubble-up sponge filters are particularly useful in breeding setups. Apart from providing gentle filtration, the sponge will be picked over regularly by small fry. This additional food source is particularly useful for catfishes and other fish that constantly browse.

Water hardness levels

The ideal water conditions for each breeding setup are described in terms of temperature, pH (degree of acidity or alkalinity) and hardness. The hardness is quoted as 'ppm', which stands for 'parts per million'. This refers to the concentration of calcium carbonate in the water (one of the substances that causes hardness) in mg per litre. Other scales, such as °dH, are also commonly used. The accepted grades of water hardness are as follows:

Very soft	0 - 50 ppm
Moderately soft	50 - 100 ppm
Slightly hard	100 - 150 ppm
Moderately hard	150 - 200 ppm
Hard	200 - 300 ppm
Very hard	300+ ppm

Coral sand can be used to harden water. This can either be placed in a filter or used as a substrate with a subgravel filter.

Water changes in fry tanks

Partial water changes are vital to the health and well-being of the youngsters. Many breeding setups have little in the way of filtration, so water changes are the only way to remove pollutants. Start by changing 10% of the water once a week and step this up as the fry grow. Providing the replacement water you use has the same pH, hardness and temperature as the tank water, you can gradually increase water changes to 50% twice weekly.

When selecting potential breeding stock, always look for fish with robust bodies, perfect finnage and good strong colours. They are the most likely to pass on these attributes to their offspring. Never breed from deformed fish; many defects will be inherited characteristics that will be passed on to the offspring and subsequent generations.

Inbreeding

Inbreeding occurs when closely related fish breed together. It is a particular problem if rigorous culling is not carried out and where there has been poor selection of breeding stock. To guard against this problem, try to obtain your stock from different sources and combine a male from one breeder or dealer with a female from another.

The exception to this rule is where you are working with a cultivated fish, such as guppies. In this case, obtain all your stock from one breeder and seek advice about how to manage them genetically over successive generations.

Hybridisation

A hybrid is created when two species breed together. Many of our most beautiful garden plants are hybrids, and much of what we eat, both vegetable and animal, is of hybrid origin. In the aquatic world, all the colourful livebearers and discus strains have their roots in skilful hybridisation, followed by years of selective breeding.

The main problem with hybridisation arises when offspring are passed on to other aquarists as a true species. Also, indiscriminate hybridisation often occurs in mixed Malawi cichlid tanks. Any fry from such a setup must be viewed with some suspicion.

Deliberate hybridisation between two species 'just to see what comes out' is usually a waste of time, as nearly all the offspring from such matings look like a 'halfway house' between the parent species. You might as well enjoy breeding the true species and have worthwhile youngsters to pass on to other aquarists.

The rearing tank

One important factor that is often overlooked is the size of the rearing tank. Contrary to what you might imagine, it is not a case of the larger the better; small fry seem to do better in smaller tanks. As they grow you can move them into larger tanks. Ultimately, this seems to produce bigger and better fish.

It is important to remember that as the fish mature, they may not be happy in a large group of their own kind. Cichlids start to fight and look for mates, Siamese fighter males will kill each other, and so on. Try to move youngsters on so that you only keep back a small group as potential breeders for your next generation.

Rearing the offspring

To obtain good-quality young fish, you need to follow a few simple rules. First and foremost, never crowd the fry. Whilst small fry do better in a smaller aquarium because it is easier for them to find food, as they grow, you must move them to larger quarters. A large brood of young may number hundreds of fish, but the tank you are rearing them

in will only cope with about 30 adults. At some point, the young will start to become stunted. Only by splitting the fry into several tanks can you rear most of the fry. Alternatively, you will have to cull the surplus young, which can be distressing, but without it all the young will suffer and may die.

If you do have to cull excess fry, this is best done when the babies are very young. In many ways it is probably best to follow nature and scoop out the surplus fry and release them into an aquarium with large adult fish. Alternatively, you can obtain some anaesthetic from your veterinarian and use that to put the surplus babies to sleep.

Spawning mops

Spawning mops are really useful pieces of equipment and yet one of the few items generally not for sale in an aquarium dealer. They are the ideal alternative to live plants because they can be properly sterilised before being used in a breeding setup. They can be any size or density and be placed exactly where the fish want to spawn.

Most aquarists make their own spawning mops out of nylon wool. Green is the preferred colour because it looks more natural. To make a spawning mop, take this book and wind the wool around the shorter side until you have about 30 strands, then cut off the surplus. Using a 20cm (8in) piece of wool, tie the strands together. Turn over the book and cut the wool strands at a point opposite your knot. You now have a spawning mop. Wash this under the tap in warm (not boiling) water and it is ready to use. For larger mops, use the longer side of the book and wind about 40 strands around it. If the mop is to hang from the surface you can attach it to a polystyrene float or cork. Before reusing a mop, always dry it out completely and wash it in hot, but not boiling, water.

Making a spawning mop

1 Wind green nylon wool around a piece of card or the short side of this book until you have about 30 strands. Cut off the surplus.

2 Cut another piece of wool about 20cm (8in) long from the ball and thread it under the strands. Secure the strands with a tight knot.

3 Turn over the card or book and cut the wool strands at a point opposite your knot. You now have your spawning mop.

Do not cut off the long ends of the wool securing the strands.

4 The long ends of wool securing the mop strands can be used to tie the mop to a cork or to suspend it from the surface of the aquarium.

No matter how good it is, flake food is generally not enough to bring fish into breeding condition. You must add live foods or their frozen equivalent to the diet. These are available in various forms and most aquatic dealers sell at least one type of live food. You can collect live daphnia from ponds without any fish living in them and culture whiteworms and grindalworms as conditioning foods. When conditioning large fish, offer them bloodworms (available from aquatic stores) and chopped earthworms from the garden. Feed those fish that need vegetable matter in their diet on blanched lettuce, spinach or peas.

Breeding stock should be fed at least three times a day. Make sure that all the food is eaten within five minutes (live food can be left longer) and try to space out the meals throughout the day. A good routine is to offer one feed first thing in the morning, a second in the late afternoon or early evening, and a final feed an hour before you go to bed.

Feeding the young

Baby fish need feeding more often than adults, so try to feed them at least three times a day or, better still, five times. Ground-up adult flake food is not a suitable food for young fish. They need a higher protein content in their diet and will be stunted if this is all you offer them. Buy fry and growth foods to feed your fish fry and supplement these products with some live food. Certain live foods are very useful for rearing young fry. Here is a selection of the most important ones.

Infusoria This is a general term used for many different microscopic organisms that live in water and feed on rotting plant matter. The spores are airborne, so you do not need a starter culture, only a suitable medium and food. Take an open jar of aquarium water and drop in a piece of lightly boiled potato. After about a week, the water will be cloudy with infusoria. To feed the fry, just pour some of the cloudy water into the tank and top up the jar with fresh aquarium water. Having about five cultures on the go at any one time should keep your fry supplied with infusoria.

Daphnia (water fleas)

Bloodworms (red midge larvae)

Brineshrimp

Left: *To establish a supply of infusoria to feed young fry, place a piece of lightly boiled potato in a jar of old aquarium water and leave it open to the air.*

Below: *Keep the jar in a warm, moderately lit spot and after about a week the water will be cloudy with infusoria. Simply pour some into the tank.*

Brineshrimp Newly hatched brineshrimp is the next fry food. Many species can take it as a first food, but it is always wise to feed a little infusoria to start with, as well as brineshrimp. That way, if the fry are not big enough to handle the larger food, they will not starve to death.

Dried brineshrimp eggs are available from many aquatic outlets. They are supplied in sealed cans or small glass containers and must be kept dry in a cool room or refrigerator. This is very important if you buy a large can and feed only small amounts, It may take many months or even a year to use up all the eggs. If you keep them in damp or warm conditions, they will fail to hatch after a few months.

Hatching brineshrimp eggs is easy. Half fill a one-litre plastic drinks bottle with fresh tapwater and add one and a half teaspoons of sea salt. Add a quarter of a teaspoon of eggs and drop

Well washed plastic drinks bottle, with airline shown below.

Use aquarium salt rather than table salt.

The eggs are like fine sand grains. Use only a small quantity at a time.

in an airline attached to an airpump; the bubbles will circulate the eggs in the bottle. After about 36 hours at 24°C (75°F), the eggs will have hatched and you can take out the airline. The shrimps collect at the bottom and the shells float to the surface. After a further 30 minutes, siphon out the shrimps with some airline and filter them through a paper towel. Wash them in freshwater and feed them to the fry.

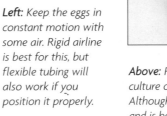

Left: Keep the eggs in constant motion with some air. Rigid airline is best for this, but flexible tubing will also work if you position it properly.

Below: Remove the airline after 36 hours. The shrimps gather near the bottom, swimming with a jerky motion. Siphon them into another container.

Above: Place a spoonful of the old microworm culture on the surface of the new medium. Although this is a good food, it can be smelly and is best kept well away from the kitchen.

Microworms These excellent little worms can be fed instead of, or as well as, brineshrimp. You will need to obtain a starter culture from another aquarist and set up your own cultures from it.

The worms feed on the surface of cereal-based foods such as porridge. To make a culture medium, simply cook up a little porridge in the normal way – but using only water – and allow it to cool. Place a layer about 1cm (0.4in) thick on the bottom of a clean plastic tub. Take a small spoonful of the old culture and tip it on top of the new one. Put the lid on the container (with some air holes punched in it) and keep it in a warm place. A few days later, there will be so many worms that there is not enough room on the surface for them all and they start climbing up the sides of the container. Wipe them off the sides and feed them directly to your fry. Keep a succession of cultures under way, as they go off after about a week.

This group of fish contains a huge range of species, including many popular aquarium subjects, such as barbs, danios, loaches, minnows, rasboras and 'sharks'. They range in size from fish that are fully grown at only 2.5cm (1in) to fish that may achieve a size in excess of 2m (6.5ft). Most members of this suborder are omnivores and will take a wide range of foods. Some species have barbels that they use to search through the substrate for anything edible.

Cyprinids form the backbone of the ornamental fish-farming industry and contain both species ranked as very easy beginner fish to breed and others that are considered problem fish. On the whole, they are egg-scatterers that broadcast spawn into plants. Some species produce adhesive or semi-adhesive eggs that become entangled in plant fronds and develop there for a day or two before hatching – many rasboras spawn in this way. Other species, including most barbs and danios, produce non-adhesive eggs that fall onto the substrate and develop there. A few place their adhesive eggs in specific locations and may even practise brood care. Of these, one of the more commonly available species is the fathead minnow *(Pimephales promelas promelas)*, which lays its eggs onto the underside of a rock or overhanging branch. Once spawning is complete, the male drives off the original female and protects his nest from allcomers. Other ripe females may be allowed to spawn into his nest site, so several batches of eggs may develop together. The eggs take about five days to hatch, at which time the fry are 5mm (0.2in) long and, once they are free-swimming, can take newly hatched brineshrimp.

Right: Cherry barbs like to spawn into a clump of fine-leaved plants and tend to return to the same spot time and again to mate. In between matings, they will swim around much of the aquarium, with the male displaying to his mate and chasing her about.

Typical spawning setup

With such a wide diversity within the group, it is very difficult to describe a typical spawning setup for these fish. However, it is clear that most of them are egg-scatterers that eat their own eggs after spawning, so provide large clumps of plants or artificial spawning mops as refuges for the eggs. Remove the adults as soon as possible after spawning.

Water quality will depend very much on where the species originated, so do some detective work to ensure that you recreate the natural conditions properly. As a general rule, most commonly kept

Left: Each species tends to spawn in a set pattern, but not always. These are the developing eggs of harlequins. This fish usually spawns on the underside of a broad leaf, but sometimes lays its eggs into fine-leaved plants, as here.

cyprinids seem happier spawning in soft water, with a neutral to slightly acidic pH rather than hard, alkaline water. Hard water can cause the eggshells of some sensitive species to harden to the point where the youngster cannot break free and all the eggs of a spawning die before hatching. For this reason, it is usually best to use soft water if you are not sure of a particular species' requirements.

Many authorities suggest using two or three males for each female, but what tends to happen is that only one male takes part in the spawning and the others just go round eating any eggs they can find. Select the strongest and most robust pair and only place those two individuals into the spawning tank.

Since most spawnings occur early in the day, it is a good idea to place the potential breeders in your spawning tank last thing at night. This should be after a period of conditioning, during which the males and females have been kept separate and fed on plenty of live foods.

Many cyprinids seem to be stimulated to spawn by early morning sunlight, so position the aquarium where it will receive direct sun first thing in the morning. This is by no means essential, but it does seem to help.

Once the fry are beyond the infusoria stage, add a small bubble-up sponge filter to the aquarium to help maintain the water quality. Carry out 10% water changes every week, but because the small fry are very delicate, make sure that the fresh water is the same temperature and does not contain any chlorine or chloramines. When the fry are 2.5cm (1in) long, step up the aquarium filtration and perform larger water changes.

Left: *Cryptocorynes are excellent broadleaved plants for the spawning tank. They can tolerate poor lighting much better than many other species and do well when grown in a pot.*

Below: *Cabomba is an ideal fine-leaved plant that many cyprinids love to spawn into. The one problem with it is that it tends to fall to pieces within a few weeks, but this is long enough for the eggs to hatch out.*

Below: *Java moss makes an excellent spawning plant. It forms large, dense clumps into which eggs can fall, and many species like to dive into when spawning. It also helps to keep the water pure by removing pollutants.*

Cabomba is usually sold in bunches with a lead weight wrapped around the bottom of the stems. Remove this and wash the plants in clean water, otherwise you risk introducing pests into the breeding tank.

African barbs are considered more difficult to breed than their Asian counterparts, probably because most Asian barbs are mass-produced for the hobby, whereas most African species are wild-caught. Many African barbs are seasonal spawners and difficult to breed at the wrong time of year. Most spawnings occur in autumn and early winter, when river levels are higher and food more plentiful.

Before attempting to spawn them, place the adults in single-sex tanks and condition them well on plenty of live foods for several weeks. Select the plumpest female and liveliest male and move them into the spawning setup. Courtship is usually triggered at first light, but mating occurs several hours later. The pair dive into the spawning mop or clump of plants and press their bodies together as they release eggs and milt. The clear non-adhesive eggs are scattered as the pair break away and are ignored as courtship and further pairings take place over the next hour or two. Remove the parents immediately after spawning, otherwise they will eat any eggs they find. Eggs hatch after 36 hours and fry are free-swimming on the third day.

Sex differences

Unless the fish are fully mature, this is a difficult species to sex. Males are slimmer than females and often have a hint of red in their fins. Females full of eggs are quite noticeable.

Left: *The slimmer fish is the male. The pair will need more conditioning before you can attempt to spawn them.*

Rearing the fry

Newly born fry are rather small and need infusoria or a liquid fry food for at least a week before they are ready to move on to microworms and brineshrimp. Once on this diet they grow quickly and can reach 2.5cm (1in) in 10 weeks. Regular 10% water changes are essential once the fry are feeding on microworms, etc. Step them up to 25% weekly when the young are a couple of months old. Use a bubble-up sponge filter initially, then an internal power filter when the fry are 2.5cm (1in) long.

Breeding setup

Moderately soft, neutral to slightly acidic water, up to 100 ppm and pH 6.5-7.

Tank measuring 60x30x30cm (24x12x12in).

Set the temperature at 24-27°C (75-80°F).

Cover the base with artificial spawning mops or large clumps of Java moss.

CHERRY BARB • *Barbus titteya*

This Asian barb spawns in much the same way as nearly all other Asian species. Condition the adults separately and after a couple of weeks, place a plump female with a brightly coloured male into the breeding tank. If you do this late in the evening, most pairs will start spawning soon after.

Courtship is initiated by the male early in the morning. It usually starts with him lazily chasing his mate around the aquarium, but gradually speeds up as he starts flaring his fins and performing a courtship dance in front of her. Eventually, he entices her to a particular area of plant cover in, or just above, which the pair mate. This involves them turning over on their sides or even upside down, with the male's fins wrapped over the female's body. About five eggs are released with each embrace and these hang by a sticky thread from the plant fronds. Spawning may take several hours, but once complete, the pair will start to cruise around eating any eggs they can find. Remove the parents swiftly to give the eggs a chance of surviving until they can hatch a day later. The fry are not free-swimming until the third day; at this time they look like slivers of glass and tend to congregate near plants or under the water surface.

Rearing the fry

The fry are very small and require a liquid fry food or infusoria for a week before moving on to newly hatched brineshrimp, microworms and powdered fry food.

Keep a close lookout for signs of velvet disease as the fry grow up. This condition can be easily cured if caught early on. Partial water changes and gradually changing the water chemistry until conditions become moderately hard and alkaline will help to prevent the onset of the disease.

Breeding setup

Clean, slightly acidic water (up to 200 ppm and pH 6.8). Allow it to stand for a few days before adding the fish.

Position the tank where it will receive early morning sunlight.

Tank measuring 60x30x30cm (24x12x12in).

Plenty of bunches of fine-leaved plants or artificial spawning mops.

Set the temperature at 26-27°C (79-80°F).

No substrate

Left: Here, a ripe female cherry barb is about to spawn with her brighter coloured mate. Some males can be an even deeper red colour.

Sex differences

As immature fish, both sexes are a very similar pale pink colour. However, as they mature, males develop a beautiful bright scarlet colour throughout most of the body.

17

ZEBRA and LEOPARD DANIOS • *Brachydanio rerio*

Zebra danios are often recommended as a good fish for novice breeders to spawn. In fact, because the fry are so small, they are more difficult than many other species.

Place a well-conditioned pair in the aquarium just before you turn out the lights. Most pairs spawn the following morning. This tends to be a frenetic affair, with the male chasing his mate around at breakneck speed. Eventually, they join in a spawning embrace in which they twist into an S-shape. Non-adhesive eggs fall down into the substrate. Remove the adults as soon as they finish spawning. An adult pair can produce up to 400 eggs, which take up to four days to hatch.

Silver and blue stripes indicate that this is a female.

Right: *Pairs tend to spawn just above the substrate, often next to a clump of plants.*

Sex differences

Although superficially different, zebra and leopard danios are the same species and can be sexed in the same way. Males have an overall golden background colour, while females are more silver. Body shape is also a good indicator, since females tend to be much plumper than males.

Breeding setup

Tank measuring 60x30x30cm (24x12x12in).

Water hardness and pH not critical.

Several bunches of fine-leaved plants and some gentle aeration.

Set the temperature at 23-26°C (73-79°F).

Cover the base with large pea gravel or a double layer of glass marbles.

Rearing the fry

The fry become free-swimming on the seventh day, at which time they need infusoria or a liquid fry food. It may be a week before they are large enough to eat newly hatched brineshrimp, although they can usually tackle microworms after a couple of days. Add a bubble-up sponge filter to the setup in the third week and start 10% water changes at four weeks. The young can reach a length of 2.5cm (1in) in only eight weeks.

RAINBOW DACE • *Cyprinella lutrensis*

Since these are seasonal spawners, wait until mid-spring before attempting any spawning, and condition the adults well for several weeks. It is wise to separate the sexes before making any spawning attempt, but since they are only happy in a shoal, make sure you have six or more of each sex. Once in the breeding setup, they should spawn the following day, but if not, leave them for another day or two before removing them and trying an alternative pair.

Courtship occurs about two hours after first light and may continue for several hours before greyish white eggs are deposited between the rocks in batches of up to 30. As the parents are very likely to eat them, even between matings, be sure to feed the adults very well before the spawning attempt and remove them as soon as possible afterwards.

Sex differences

Males are more brightly coloured (particularly during the breeding season) and develop breeding tubercles (small raised white spots) on the pectoral fins and head. Females fill up with roe from mid-spring and will breed periodically for several months from late spring onwards. In captivity, spawnings as late as mid-autumn have been recorded.

Left: *A group of males. The lower fish, with breeding tubercles and better colour, is the best choice for spawning. Place him together with the plumpest female in the breeding setup.*

Rearing the fry

The eggs hatch after 40 hours and the youngsters are free-swimming within five days. They need infusoria as a first food, but can usually manage newly hatched brineshrimp within three days. At this stage add a bubble-up sponge filter to the setup and carry out 10% water changes every week. Once the young are about 2.5cm (1in) long, include an internal power filter and change 25% of the water weekly.

Breeding setup

Provide gentle aeration.

Moderately hard, slightly alkaline water. Water hardness and pH not critical.

Provide some areas of thick plant cover. Java moss is ideal for this species.

Tank measuring 90x30x30cm (36x12x12in).

Set the temperature at 23°C (73°F).

Plenty of rockwork and bogwood.

Sandy substrate

COOLIE LOACH • *Pangio kuhlii*

The coolie loach seems more likely to spawn when kept as a group rather than in individual pairs. Three to five pairs works well; since there are several subspecies or colour forms, it is important to make sure that they are all of the same type.

This is a secretive species and few people have actually observed it spawning. Courtship certainly includes the male gently mouthing a female around her vent. The pair wrap around each other and entwine at this stage, before swimming off and finding an area of thick plant growth near the surface. Here they join together side by side and whilst pressing against each other, release eggs and sperm. The eggs are green for camouflage. Several pairs may spawn together or individually.

As soon as you are sure that there has been breeding activity (the females will look a lot slimmer), remove the adults.

Above: *Coolie loaches love a well-planted tank, where they can scuttle about rooting out any morsels that have fallen between the fronds.*

Rearing the fry

It can be very difficult to find any fry in the early stages of development; in fact, the first time most aquarists realise that their coolie loaches have bred is when they find miniature replicas of the adults – and these of course are the lucky survivors of natural spawnings that have taken place in a community aquarium. In a controlled situation, you can assume that you will have several hundred fry. Feed them microworms and newly hatched brineshrimp. Within a few weeks you will be able to see some of the youngsters out and about, even during daylight hours.

Breeding setup

Since this species tends to spawn in surface plants, include thick plant cover in this area of the aquarium. Use plants that develop a good rootstock below the water surface, such as water lettuce (Pistia stratiotes), instead of plants such as duckweed.

Tank measuring 60x30x30cm (24x12x12in).

Water lettuce (Pistia stratiotes)

Soft, acidic water (below 50 ppm) and pH 6.0-6.5).

Include plenty of plants, tubes and caves for the adults to hide in.

Set the temperature at 24-27°C (75-80°F).

Scissortail rasboras were originally imported with a shipment of harlequins. This happy accident gave us one of the most popular rasboras in the hobby.

Place a well-conditioned pair into the tank late one evening and they should start spawning first thing the following morning. After each pairing (which usually takes place above or next to a suspended mop), a batch of clear eggs drifts slowly downwards. Over several hours, more than 150 eggs will be produced, although large adults may lay many more than this. It is said that this species can grow up to 20cm (8in) in the wild and that fish this size can produce over 1500 eggs in one spawning, but since it is rare to find wild-caught fish in the aquarium hobby, such large fish are never seen these days. Remove the adults as soon as possible after spawning, otherwise they will eat any eggs they find.

Sex differences

Males are more slender and tend to remain smaller. Otherwise, this species can be difficult to sex until the fish are fully mature.

Right: It will be several more months before these attractive scissortail rasboras can be sexed with any certainty.

Breeding setup

Tank measuring 60x30x30cm (24x12x12in).

Suspend a few mops from the surface at one end of the tank.

Set the temperature at 24-27°C (75-80°F).

Very soft, acidic water (less than 50 ppm and pH 5.5-6.0). Rainwater filtered through carbon and allowed to stand for a week or so with waterlogged peat in it should produce the correct readings.

Cover the bottom with artificial spawning mops.

Rearing the fry

The eggs take two days to hatch and the fry are free-swimming on the fourth day. At this stage, they are just about large enough to handle newly hatched brineshrimp, but feed them some infusoria or a liquid fry food as well to be on the safe side. A week after the fry are well and truly feeding on brineshrimp, you can introduce gentle filtration. At a month old, they should be large enough to cope with 10% water changes. If the brood is large, make sure you spread them out into several aquariums, otherwise they will quickly become stunted.

21

WHITE CLOUD MOUNTAIN MINNOW • *Tanichthys albonubes*

White Cloud Mountain minnows were once known as 'poor man's neons' and this old name shows just how brightly coloured youngsters of this species are.

Place an adult, well-conditioned pair in the breeding aquarium late in the evening. Most pairs that have not seen the opposite sex for a few weeks will spawn the following morning, but some strains seem to produce small batches of eggs over a longer period of time and may take a few days to start spawning. Spawning is initiated by the male and includes much fin-flaring. Pairs spawn into plants or artificial mops and during the embrace, males will completely wrap themselves around their partner. Up to 20 eggs may be produced in a single embrace, but five is a more usual number. Once spawning is complete, it is a good idea to remove the adults.

Breeding setup

Tank measuring 60x30x30cm (24x12x12in).

Set the temperature at 22°C (72°F).

Water hardness and pH not critical.

Some floating plants are also useful.

Position the aquarium where it will receive early morning sunlight.

Provide plenty of clumps of fine-leaved plants or artificial spawning mops.

Sex differences

Males are much brighter coloured and slimmer than females. Older males often develop a 'pigeon chest' and may look like females from the side, but they never have the girth of a true female. Since there are several different colour forms of this fish in the hobby, try to locate a strain with strong, bright coloration for spawning. A long-finned version is also available.

This mature male may develop a pigeon chest as he gets older.

Left: *Ripe females are usually plumper than this female before spawning. Good feeding with live foods will help bring her into spawning condition.*

Rearing the fry

The eggs hatch in two days and become free-swimming on the third. Fry require infusoria or liquid fry food as a first food, but brineshrimp can follow from about the fifth day onwards. Before discontinuing smaller foods, check that the babies' stomachs are pink when they have fed on newly hatched brineshrimp. White Cloud Mountain minnows grow very rapidly and look like young neon tetras when they are 1.25cm (0.5in) long.

The scientific name of the harlequin rasbora has recently been changed from *Rasbora heteromorpha* to *Trigostoma heteromorpha*. Despite this, most retailers still use the old scientific name.

Place a well-conditioned adult male with a younger plump female in the aquarium late in the evening. Courtship is instigated by the male and includes the usual fin-flaring and dancing in front of his intended mate. The pair start swimming around the tank together and eventually move underneath a suitable leaf. Here they turn upside down and deposit a few eggs. Then they move off and court some more before coming back to spawn again (usually in the same general area). Occasionally, they deposit eggs above fine-leaved plants, but this is rare when they are given a choice. About 40 eggs are deposited in an average spawning and although the adults are not rabid egg-eaters, they should still be removed as soon as possible afterwards.

Right: This pair of harlequin rasboras is spawning upside down under a leaf. Some pairs will spawn right side up instead, or even into fine-leaved plants. The female is the nearest fish.

Sex differences

Males have redder fins than females and the rear portion of their body is a more intense red. Females are also deeper and fuller in the body when they are in breeding condition.

Breeding setup

Tank measuring 60x30x30cm (24x12x12in).

Very soft and moderately acidic water (up to 50 ppm and pH 6.0).

Also provide a few clumps of fine-leaved plants, such as cabomba.

Set up a thickly planted area using broadleaved plants, such as these cryptocorynes.

Sand or fine gravel substrate.

Set the temperature at 27°C(80°F).

Rearing the fry

The eggs hatch the following day and the fry are free-swimming on the third day. Give them infusoria or liquid fry foods for a week before feeding them on brineshrimp. From here on, they grow very quickly and will reach 2.5cm (1in) in only three months. Add a bubble-up sponge filter once the fry are feeding on brineshrimp, and after a month start changing 10% of the water on a weekly basis.

Characins are a very old group of fish that evolved before the continents started to break up, so there are representatives both in Africa and in Central and South America. This has allowed the fish plenty of time to evolve different reproductive strategies depending on their needs, and most aquarists think they are all egg-scatterers that do not care for their young; how wrong they are!

The most famous characin of all is the red piranha (*Serrasalmus nattereri*). Males of this species dig a pit in the substrate and entice a female to lay her eggs in it. Initially, both parents guard them, but after a day the male chases her away and looks after the eggs and newborns himself. Other characins lay their eggs in different substrates. Many pyrrhulina spawn on plant leaves underwater, while their close cousins the splashing tetras (*Copella arnoldi*)

spawn on the underside of a plant leaf, above the water surface. To do this the pair carefully position themselves under the leaf and jump out of the water together. They flip over as they fly through the air and hit their target side by side upside down. A few seconds later they flip away back into the water. The male splashes his nest of eggs from time to time to keep them moist until they hatch.

Some characins are half way along the road to being livebearers, as they have adapted to fertilise their eggs internally. A few hours later, the female expels her eggs into fine-leaved plants, well away from any other fish. The swordtail characin (*Corynopoma riisei*) is one of the species that has evolved in this way.

There are many hundreds of species of characin yet to be described by science and many more than this that have yet to be kept by aquarists. From the

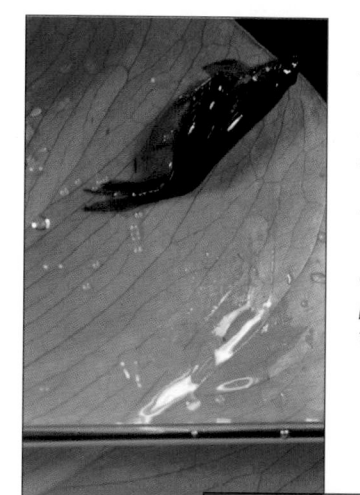

Left: Watching splashing tetras spawn is an amazing sight. Here we can see the moment of mating, when the fish expel their eggs and milt. You can see the clear eggs from previous pairings all around the mating fish.

Left: A beautiful young male splashing tetra. He is old enough to spawn, but has yet to develop his full finnage (the dorsal fin will grow longer) and body depth. In another two months he will be at his peak.

Right: A newly hatched splashing tetra baby. It has yet to free itself of the eggshell, but its tail has broken through. At this stage it will be wriggling around all the time.

ranks of these rare and unknown fish no doubt more unusual reproductive strategies will be discovered.

In general, characins live in soft acidic water and many species need these conditions if their eggs are to hatch. Eggs laid in hard water absorb some of the minerals into their shells, which become too hard for the embryos to break open. These embryos are still alive and develop until the point at which they would normally hatch, before dying off.

Java fern makes a good spawning medium. It also survives for long periods in poor light conditions and will form a clump on the substrate for fry to hide in.

Another problem is sensitivity to bright light. Many characins live in water that is stained a deep brown and choose spawning sites in deep shade. Here, the eggs stand less chance of being seen and a larger percentage survive to hatch. It has been found that the eggs of some species, including neon and cardinal tetras, have become so sensitive to bright light that the embryos will die if exposed to it during their development.

Typical spawning setup

For most species, a 60x30x30cm (24x12x12in) aquarium is ample. Waterlogged peat not only provides a dark substrate that will help reduce the light reaching the eggs, but also makes it more difficult for the adults to find any eggs to eat. Since most species of characin kept by aquarists are typical egg-scatterers, a general breeding setup should include material on which the pair can lay their eggs. A large clump of Java moss works well, as would several artificial spawning mops suspended from the water surface. They are large enough to reach right down to the substrate. Set the temperature at 77°F (25°C). Very soft water is essential (see page 8 for details of how to filter and soften rainwater).

For most egg-scatterers, it is a good idea to separate the sexes for a week or two and feed them plenty of live foods during this period. This allows the females to build up a batch of eggs before spawning and brings the males into spawning condition. Add them to the breeding setup late one evening and they will usually breed the next day.

Right: The soft, tea-coloured waters of the Rio Negro in the Amazon Basin are home to a wide range of characins. To breed them successfully in the home aquarium, add peat to the water to recreate these conditions.

EMPEROR TETRA • *Nematobrycon palmeri*

Emperor tetras are typical egg-scattering characins and the breeding method described here can be applied to most other species that spawn this way. Since this species is not an avid egg- or fry-eater, you can leave the adults in the aquarium until fry are seen. This is one species that is best spawned in a group, with two males and four females in the breeding setup.

Courtship and spawning take place a few hours after first light. In captivity, most spawnings take place shortly after the adults have been fed. Males instigate courtship with fin-flaring and displaying in front of a plump female. The pair then start to chase about and eventually join together next to the spawning medium. Most of the semi-adhesive eggs they expel fall into the substrate. They hatch in two days and the fry are free-swimming on the fourth day.

Above: *A beautiful young pair of emperor tetras – the female is the upper fish. Males become deeper-chested as they grow older.*

Breeding setup

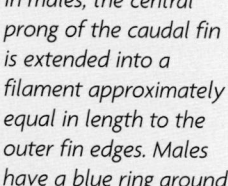

Water temperature 25°C (77°F).

Tank measuring 60x30x30cm (24x12x12in).

Use a large clump of Java moss or a mop as a spawning medium.

Very soft water is essential (up to 75 ppm maximum, pH 6.5 or lower).

Waterlogged peat substrate

Rearing the fry

Newly hatched fry congregate around a spawning mop or among the fronds of Java moss. By lifting these up on a regular basis you will see a few fry darting about. Remove the adults at this stage and feed the young on a liquid fry food. Squirt a few drops of this directly at the spawning medium every day. A little newly hatched brineshrimp can also be fed at this time. A week after the first fry are seen, all the young will be large enough to take brineshrimp.

Start 10% water changes after a few weeks. Once the fry are large enough to be easily seen, also siphon out part of the peat substrate each week. From now on use your normal tapwater for topping up.

NEON TETRA • *Paracheirodon innesi*

Neons have the reputation of being difficult to breed, when in fact they spawn very regularly in most community tanks. It is hatching and rearing the fry that is more tricky.

Add a pair to a breeding tank after conditioning them separately on plenty of live foods for a week. Courtship may start the next day at about noon, but most fish spawn on the second or even third day. Males start driving females around the aquarium, and spawning takes place in open water above the clump of Java moss, with both fish pointing directly upwards as the eggs are expelled. Remove the adults and cover the top of the aquarium with black card to exclude as much light as possible. Fry hatch in 24 hours but take a few days to become free-swimming.

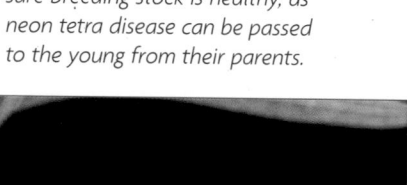

Above: *A healthy male fish. Make sure breeding stock is healthy, as neon tetra disease can be passed to the young from their parents.*

Sex differences

Mature females are larger and plumper than males, but as youngsters it is impossible to sex them reliably. Buy a shoal of eight youngsters and rear them up to be sure of obtaining both sexes.

Breeding setup

Water temperature 25°C (77°F). Very soft water (up to 25 ppm maximum, pH 6 or lower).

Tank measuring 60x30x30cm (24x12x12in).

Paint or cover the back and sides with black and position the tank away from direct light.

Rearing the fry

Feed infusoria or a liquid fry food for the first week to 10 days, after which the fry will be able to take newly hatched brineshrimp. They are greedy feeders and it is possible for them to gorge themselves to the point where serious internal damage occurs. They grow quickly, but are over 1cm (0.4in) long before they colour up. Asian-bred and wild-caught fish tend to produce small numbers of healthy fry, but once these have been reared up by the breeder, second generation broods can number up to 400 healthy young.

Above: *A plump female in breeding condition. If well fed, a female like this will spawn every week, producing between 50 and 100 eggs per spawning.*

Provide Java moss as a spawning medium.

Waterlogged peat substrate

HOCKEY STICK PENCILFISH • *Nannostomus eques*

Hockey stick pencilfish are very distinctive fish that rest at a 45-60° angle in the water column. Even small fry just a few weeks old do this.

Select a plump female and the brightest coloured, most active male as potential breeders and place them in the aquarium during the evening. Most well-conditioned pairs spawn in a few days. Courtship involves much fin-flaring and chasing about the aquarium. Eventually, the pair select the underside of a Java fern leaf on which to deposit their eggs, but few of these adhere to this surface; most just fall onto the peat substrate. Once spawning is complete, remove the adults. The fry hatch in a day or two, but take up to two more days before they start to feed on infusoria.

Left: At 1.8cm (0.7in), youngsters have developed their full adult coloration, but they are not sexable at this size. Given enough room and good feeding, they become sexually mature by eight months of age, at which time they will be 5cm (2in) long.

Rearing the fry

The fry are very small and need infusoria for at least a week before progressing to larger foods. Once on these they grow faster, but are still only 2.5cm (1in) long at about four months of age.

Right: A well-conditioned pair of hockey stick pencilfish. The female is the lower fish. They would probably spawn every week if well fed.

Sex differences

Females are plumper and less brightly coloured. In males, the anal fin is rounded at the front end, while in females it is pointed and straight-edged at the front.

Breeding setup

Tank measuring 60x30x30cm (24x12x12in).

Water temperature 25°C (77°F). Very soft water (50 ppm maximum, pH 6.5 or lower).

Provide Java fern rather than spawning mops or Java moss.

Waterlogged peat substrate

Congo tetras are one of the few African tetras to be regularly kept by aquarists. You will need a larger version of the standard setup to breed them.

Place a well-conditioned pair into the aquarium shortly before turning out the lights. Most pairs will spawn the following morning. The male instigates courtship by chasing the female up and down the aquarium and flaring his fins at her. At this time his colours are absolutely stunning. Once she is suitably aroused, they dive into a spawning mop or clump of Java moss and, shuddering side by side, release eggs and milt. The clear eggs adhere to plant fronds or fall into the peat substrate. With each dive this may become badly stirred up, but the fish don't seem to worry. Remove the adults as soon as spawning has finished. The eggs hatch in about five days.

Rearing the fry

Fry hang on to the spawning medium for a couple of days before they become free-swimming. At this time they need infusoria for a day or two before tackling newly hatched brineshrimp. Once the fry are 2cm (0.8in) long, they will take larger foods and a proprietary growth food. They are sexable at 5cm (2in), but are nearer 7.5cm (3in) before they are sexually mature.

Breeding setup

Tank measuring 90x30x45cm (36x12x18in).

Water temperature 25°C (77°F). Very soft water (up to 75 ppm maximum, pH 6.5).

Sex differences

Males have long extensions to the caudal fin and are more brightly coloured. Their dorsal fin is also extended. Females are smaller and plumper.

Alternatively, use spawning mops.

Provide Java moss as a spawning medium.

Waterlogged peat substrate

Left: *This is a young pair of congo tetras, with the male (upper fish) just beginning to develop his distinctive fin extensions.*

WEITZMAN'S SAILFIN CHARACIN • *Poecilocharax weitzmani*

As with most new aquarium fish, it was difficult at first to persuade these little gems of the characin world to spawn in captivity. Now that the method is known, it is relatively easy to succeed with these gorgeous fish.

Condition the adults well on plenty of live foods before placing them in the tank. The male will usually take up residence in the pot as soon as he is settled in his new home. The female will find a comfortable area next to the Java moss to call her own. Most days, the male will be seen courting his mate by extending his fins and flaring his black gills. A few days, or even a few weeks, later she will disappear into the male's pot with him. A batch of eggs (up to 300 from a large pair) is laid on the cave wall, after which the male guards the entrance while his mate looks after the eggs and fry. The eggs take four days to hatch and are free-swimming after another few days. They then move out of the male's cave and hide among the plants. It is a good idea to remove the adults as soon as the eggs have hatched to make sure the fry are not eaten.

Left: This young male Poecilocharax weitzmani shows the larger fins and brighter colours of his sex. As he matures, his fins will become even larger and more beautiful.

Right: This female will need plenty of live foods to bring her into spawning condition. Small worms, such as grindalworms, are ideal for this purpose, although brineshrimp have also been used.

Breeding setup

Rearing the fry

The fry need infusoria as a first food, although they can take microworms almost as soon as they leave the nest. Follow these with brineshrimp a few days to a week later. Once the fry are feeding on brineshrimp, they grow quickly and are sexable at 2.5cm (1in) long.

Tank measuring 30x20x20cm (12x8x8in).

Provide a small terracotta pot (7.5cm/3in across the base) with a hole about 3cm (1.2in) across knocked in its base. Place it upside down towards the aquarium front.

Water temperature 25°C (77°F). Very soft water is essential (below 50 ppm, pH less than 6.5).

Java moss

Waterlogged peat substrate

Small tetras such as these make excellent community fish and may even spawn in a well-planted community aquarium. Anubias plants make a good spawning medium. Amazon swordplants may be used as an alternative, but if the leaves are soft and float about too much, the fish are likely to reject them as a potential spawning site.

Place a single pair of fish in the breeding setup. If they have been kept in single-sex tanks and been well fed for a couple of weeks before the spawning attempt is made, most pairs will breed in a day or two. Courtship is long and intricate. Initially, the male cleans the leaf using his body to vibrate above it and even rub right up against it. Later, the female will come calling and a great deal of displaying by both fish takes place. Eventually they will settle down to spawning. At this time the pair join together just above the leaf, and eggs and milt are released onto the male's pelvic fin. A second later the pair break away and the fertilised eggs are allowed to drop onto the plant leaf.

Left: A pair of Pyrrhulina laeta *spawning, with the male above. His mate is in the typical S-shape that accompanies egg release.*

Above: Here we can see a batch *of eggs developing. The ones that have turned white will not hatch and were probably infertile.*

Rearing the fry

The fry are free-swimming in four days, at which time they need infusoria or a liquid fry food. After a few days on this diet, they are usually large enough to take newly hatched brineshrimp or microworms. They tend to stay together in a shoal at this stage, although this will break down as they mature.

Sex differences

Males are darker coloured than females and have a larger and more extended dorsal and upper caudal fin lobe. During courtship and spawning, the male develops a dark stripe from in front of the eye through to the caudal peduncle.

Breeding setup

Tank measuring 60x30x30cm (24x12x12in).

Position some fine-leaved plants such as cabomba towards the back and sides.

Provide large-leaved anubias plants as a spawning medium, with leaves horizontal to the substrate.

Water temperature 24°C (75°F). Very soft water is essential (below 50 ppm, pH less than 6.5).

Sandy substrate

LIVEBEARERS

Livebearing as a method of reproduction has developed independently in many families of fish. This section looks at a small selection of species from different families, each with individual requirements.

The Poeciliidae

Most of the livebearers kept by hobbyists belong to the Poeciliidae family and include fish such as platies, guppies, mollies and swordtails. There are several hundred species within this family; most will produce broods on a monthly cycle, but many others are considered extremely difficult to breed other than very occasionally and cause problems even for very experienced aquarists. The cultivated forms that are the backbone of the trade are prolific, but because they are all of hybrid origin, maintaining or creating a good-quality strain presents difficulties. However, just saving a few young and rearing them is not a problem and for this reason they are considered easy fish to breed.

Sexing fish in this family is easy, as in mature males the anal fin is modified into a copulatory organ. This rodlike structure has some holdfasts at the tip that allow males to latch onto their mates for the few seconds it takes for sperm packets to travel from one to the other. Most species can store sperm for periods of time, so more than one brood will be produced from a single mating. Many species feed their developing fry while they are inside the female, so keep expectant mothers well fed at all times.

This is a female tuxedo platy. These fish cannot certainly be sexed until they reach sexual maturity.

The fin rays of the male's gonopodium form a channel down which sperm packets are directed into the female's vent.

The Hemirhamphidae

Halfbeaks belong to the Hemirhamphidae family, the second most common group of livebearers within the trade. Once again, the anal fin is modified into a copulatory organ, but in this case, only part of the fin is used for this function. Sperm may well be stored by females for later use and, once again, fry are fed by their mother during development. Shortly before they are born, the young of many species can be seen moving inside their mother's body.

The Goodeidae

Fish belonging to the Goodeids form another very important family of livebearers. They are only found in Mexico and include some very beautiful fish. Males have a notch in their anal fin, with just the first few rays being modified into a copulatory organ. These fish cannot store sperm, so they must mate each time before they can produce a brood of young. The fry are supplied with huge amounts of food during their development and are very large at birth. Poorly fed females produce poor-quality young that may die shortly after birth.

Below: During mating, male Poeciliids (here we see a pair of Poecilia velifera) swing the gonopodium forwards and insert it in the female's vent.

Above: *The moment of birth. This female platy has been carrying her developing embryos for 22-28 days before they are ready to face the world by themselves. At this stage, all the egg yolk will have been used up.*

Above: *Once free of their mother, the babies only have a few seconds to find cover or they will be eaten in the wild. Likewise, in a community aquarium the race is on when fry are being born. It is vital to remove the mother at this time.*

The Anablepidae

Another family of livebearers commonly found in the trade is Anablepidae. It used to contain only *Anableps anableps* (four-eyes), but now includes the one-sided livebearers. Both breed in a similar way and in both cases, the male's anal fin is modified into a copulatory organ. This time, it is twisted to the left or right and is capable of some movement near the tip. Females have a scale over one side of their vent, which prevents mating from that side, so in effect they are either left- or right-sided just like the males. In the past it was thought a left-sided male had to find a right-sided female before he could mate. It is now thought that any pair can mate — it is just more difficult for, say, two right-sided fish to mate.

The Potamotrygonidae

Stingrays belong to the last commonly found family of livebearers. Both freshwater and marine species reproduce by livebearing and are among the most majestic and beautiful of all fish. The freshwater species belong to the Potamotrygonidae family. All tend to grow to about 1m (39in) in length and are generally too large for the average aquarist to keep. However, they make wonderful public aquarium subjects and are regularly bred in captivity.

Males have claspers on their pelvic fins with which they grip the female during mating. Gestation takes 20 to 23 weeks, resulting in up to six fully formed, teaplate-sized young. Even at this size, males can be distinguished by their partially developed claspers. Most species breed late in the year.

Typical breeding setup

With so many different families included in this group, it is difficult to suggest a typical breeding setup for them as a whole. Many species will flock-breed if given ample supplies of live food and plentiful plant cover in the aquarium. This is certainly true of all but the Poeciliids. This family includes some predatory fish that will eat any baby they can find. In the case of all the cultivated varieties, you must carefully select the fish that will produce the next generation. In these circumstances, individual pairs are best established in a breeding tank. Once the female looks gravid, take away the male and leave her to give birth by herself. Remove the female as soon as possible and rear the young on their own. Separate the sexes as soon as they can be told apart.

Left: *Salvinia is a good floating plant with fine roots that hang down into the water. This makes good cover for newborn fry. Simply drop the plants on the water surface of the maternity tank.*

Right: *In this sort of situation you want to try to cover the water with a floating plant. Ideally, this salvinia should be packed in so its leaves are touching all the way across the surface.*

ONE-SIDED LIVEBEARERS • *Jenynsia multidentata*

These fish are best bred as a long-term colony. In the wild they have to tolerate wide temperature swings, but in captivity, keep them at 22-27°C (72-80°F).

Once a young female becomes sexually mature, she develops an orange spot on her gonopore. During the next week or so, males will pursue and try to mate with her virtually continuously. Once the spot disappears, you know she is pregnant.

Broods take up to eight weeks to be born. During this long gestation, they are initially free-swimming in the ovarian canal and at this time, a number of youngsters are eaten by their siblings (many sharks have this stage as well). Later in the pregnancy, the female produces club-shaped processes that enter the babies' opercular cleft and fill the mouth and pharyngeal cavity. This structure provides all the nutrients the developing baby needs to grow into a youngster about 1.25cm (0.5in) long when it is born. If you look at the gill plate of newborn youngsters, you will see that one of them sticks out more than the other. This returns to normal in a few days.

Left: A pair of one-sided livebearers. The female is the upper fish and the twisted andropodium on the male can clearly be seen turning up at the tip. Females are normally twice as large as males.

Sex differences

In males, the anal fin is modified into a copulatory organ (andropodium). This hollow tube is made of the fin rays twisted around each other and covered in a sheath. Females have a normal anal fin and are larger than males when mature. As sexually mature virgins, they have an orange spot around the vent that fades after mating.

Breeding setup

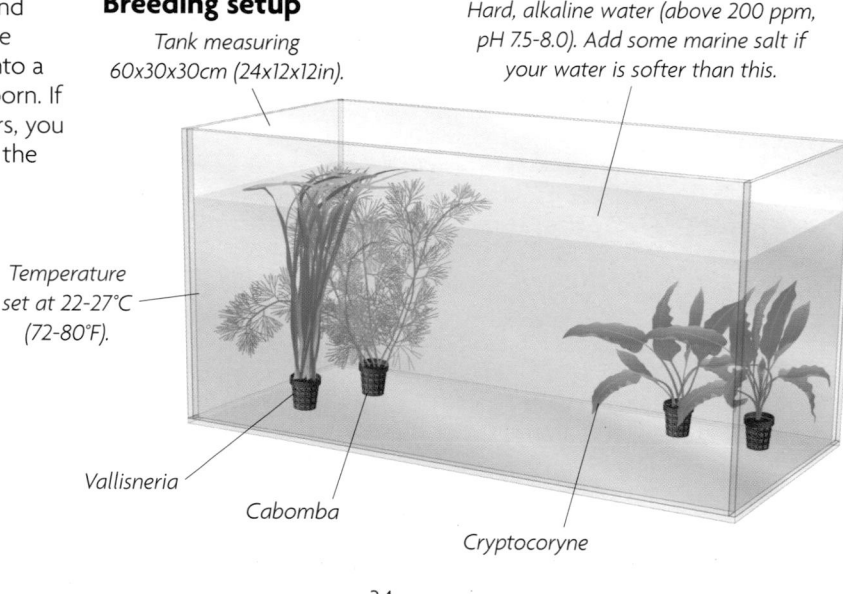

Tank measuring 60x30x30cm (24x12x12in).

Hard, alkaline water (above 200 ppm, pH 7.5-8.0). Add some marine salt if your water is softer than this.

Temperature set at 22-27°C (72-80°F).

Vallisneria

Cabomba

Cryptocoryne

Rearing the fry

Newborn fry can be attacked by hungry adults, so make sure that the whole colony is well fed. If you have a problem with cannibalism, remove any large, old females or separate gravid females when they look plump.

The fry are very large at birth and will take newly hatched brineshrimp, grindalworms, powdered fry food and even growth foods within a day or two of being born. Growth is rapid, with males developing an andropodium within four weeks of birth. They are sexually mature at about four months old.

Most cultivated mollies require large quarters, with good filtration and regular partial water changes if their environment is to remain healthy. Although they are adaptable to most water conditions, avoid very soft, acidic water. If you live in an area with this sort of tapwater, add some marine salt to the aquarium to keep the fish happy.

Females are constantly in a state of pregnancy and generally produce broods of young every four weeks. Some older females will become erratic in their breeding cycle, so it is best to use young females. Keep them with your best male, so that he fathers the next generation.

Shortly before dropping her young, most females become agitated and try to hide away from males. They are also much plumper, with a squared-off appearance. At this stage, they should be carefully removed to the breeding tank.

The fry will be born in the early hours of the morning and a large brood can number several hundred. Short-finned types tend to produce only 20-50 babies per brood. Remove the mother as soon as possible after she has given birth.

Sex differences

Males have a modified anal fin that develops shortly before they are sexually mature. In some of the larger sailfin types, this may not develop until a fish is one year old or more.

Left: A stunning pair of modern hybrid sailfin mollies. Up to four different wild species of molly were used to create these cultivated forms. The lower fish is a male, with a beautiful sail-like dorsal fin.

Breeding setup

A separate breeding tank is only needed to isolate a gravid female just before she gives birth and for rearing the youngsters. Depending upon the variety, this can be 1m (39in) or as much as 2m (78in) long. Sailfin types of mollies need as much room as possible, but short-finned varieties will do well in the smaller-sized aquarium.

Rearing the fry

Young mollies will need plenty of food if they are to achieve good growth rates. Combine a good-quality fry food with microworms, newly hatched brineshrimp and other small live foods. You can offer the fish some vegetable matter in addition to their normal diet. As they grow, feed them larger foods.

Be sure to change at least 30% of the aquarium water each week and include good filtration. A power filter can be added once the young are six weeks old. This should be capable of creating a water current for them to swim against.

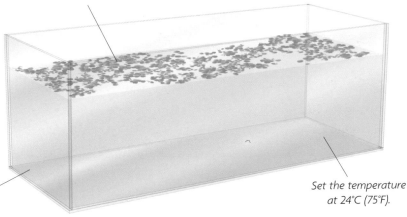

Include some floating plants, such as Salvinia natans.

Slightly hard water (above 100 ppm, pH 7.0 and above).

Set the temperature at 24°C (75°F).

These fish are best bred as a colony, so keep a group of young fish together in a 60cm (24in) aquarium with some plant cover. They are adaptable to most water conditions, but avoid extremes. Allow the temperature to fluctuate a little from summer to winter. The average summer temperature should be about 23°C (73°F), while winter temperatures should drop a few degrees to 21°C (70°F). While not as dramatic as the temperature swings these fish experience in the wild, it is enough to slow down reproduction during the winter months and allow the females a period of rest.

Feed the breeding stock on good-quality flake food, with additional feeds of live or frozen foods. Females that are ready to mate will be courted by the dominant male or two in the colony. All others are chased away by these fish. Courtship includes much fin-flaring and posturing in front of the female. When she is suitably aroused, she will shake her head from side to side to indicate that the chosen male may approach. He comes carefully alongside her and wraps his anal and dorsal fins around her body. Mating takes place and they break apart.

Gestation takes six to eight weeks, depending upon temperature. During this time the young are fed by the female through trophotaeniae (literally 'feeding worms'), which are long processes from the embryo's anus. The fry are approximately 1.25cm (0.5in) long at birth and can number up to 40 in a brood. Young females tend to produce smaller numbers of bigger fry than large old females.

Above: *This female is in the process of giving birth. The baby's tail can be seen poking out from her vent.*

Sex differences

Males have brighter colours and an enlarged dorsal fin. The first few rays of the anal fin are shortened and bunched together to form a copulatory organ.

Rearing the fry

The young like to hide in plant cover near the surface, where they will eat any small live foods they can find (newly hatched brineshrimp are a favourite food). They also appreciate additional feeds of powdered fry food followed later by growth foods. They are sexable in a little over eight weeks but do not breed them until they are 16 weeks old.

Breeding setup

Tank measuring 60x30x30cm (24x12x12in).

Slightly hard water (above 100 ppm, pH 7.0 and above).

Temperature 19-24°C (66-75°F). Provide gentle filtration.

Cabomba

Ludwigia

Amazon swords

Carry out regular partial water changes.

Individual pairs can be kept in a community aquarium until the female shows signs of being pregnant. If you have recently bought the fish, it is a good idea to let the female drop her first brood in the community aquarium rather than save them. This way, her second litter will be fathered mostly by the male you have selected.

Males tend to court females more or less constantly, fin-flaring and posturing in front of their prospective mates. However, the females seem generally uninterested in all this activity. Actual mating occurs when he attaches himself to her, using the holdfasts at the end of his gonopodium. It takes only a few seconds for sperm to be transferred and then the pair break apart. Gestation is on average 28 days, but can vary by three or four days either way. The fry are born early in the morning and hide near the bottom of the aquarium among plants. Remove the female at this time.

Breeding setup

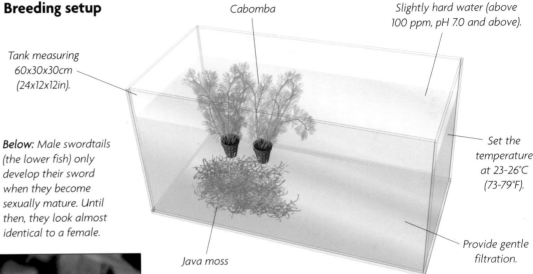

Cabomba

Slightly hard water (above 100 ppm, pH 7.0 and above).

Tank measuring 60x30x30cm (24x12x12in).

Set the temperature at 23-26°C (73-79°F).

Below: *Male swordtails (the lower fish) only develop their sword when they become sexually mature. Until then, they look almost identical to a female.*

Java moss

Provide gentle filtration.

Sex differences

Males have a modified anal fin. Females tend to be larger and have a normal anal fin. When close to term, they will have a darkened area just above their anal fin called a gravid spot. This is not visible on some strains and some males also show it.

Rearing the fry

The fry will take newly hatched brineshrimp and microworms within hours of being born. You can also feed them powdered fry foods at this time. To achieve a good growth rate, try to feed the fry at least four times a day.

The young start to sex out from about three months of age. The early sexing-out males will remain small and if left in with their sisters will father the next generation, thus passing on their genes for early maturation. For this reason, it is vital to remove these males to another tank. Once the females are six months old, select the best male to mate with the best female. This way, strains are improved rather than weakened by inbreeding.

LABYRINTHFISHES

Labyrinths are a fascinating group of fish from Africa and Asia. The group currently contains five families, 18 genera, with a total of just over 80 species. Several genera occur in Africa, but these tend to be large predatory fish, most of which are not suitable for a community aquarium. It is the Asian species that attract most attention from aquarists now, including many popular aquarium fish such as Siamese fighters, blue gouramis, dwarf gouramis and the first 'tropical' fish to be kept in captivity, the paradisefish (*Macropodus opercularis*).

From the point of view of breeding, labyrinthfishes can be divided into two main groups: mouthbrooders and those that build a bubblenest (although some species produce little or no bubblenest). Most look after their eggs and young, but some just scatter their eggs under the water surface and swim off.

Bubblenesters

Most bubblenesters build their nest at the surface, often incorporating pieces of plant to give it more stability. However, some species build a nest under a plant leaf or in a cave. Just where a fish will build its nest is mostly down to species preference, but these are intelligent fish and certain individuals may choose to spawn in a different location if they think their eggs or young stand a better chance of survival.

The larger species of gourami (pearls, moonlights, golds and blues) can produce huge broods of young, which can cause rearing problems. Broods of more than 2000 have been known and clearly, the average hobbyist cannot hope to rear them all. If you try,

they will be stunted and may end up polluting their water to the point where most of them are poisoned by their own wastes.

Mouthbrooders

The mouthbrooders are nowhere near as prolific. Brood numbers are never more than about 20 and most species produce fewer than that. This means that the fish tend to command a high price and be more difficult to find in aquarium shops. They mostly belong to the *Betta* genus and it is the males that look after the youngsters. A pair will usually spawn near the bottom of the aquarium. After the typical embrace, the female collects up the eggs and spits them at the male. He carefully takes each egg into his mouth and holds it in a pouch in his throat. There they have a regular flow of oxygenated water and are safe from predators. The fry are very large when they are released and it is thought that the male secretes a substance on which the fry feed inside the pouch before they are released.

Above: A pair of thick-lipped gouramis (Colisa labiosa) spawning. During this embrace, the female releases a stream of more than 50 eggs. After 15 to 20 more embraces, it is possible that this pair will have produced up to 1,000 eggs in a single spawning.

Typical spawning setup

Aquarium size will depend upon the species being bred, but the larger gouramis require a tank at least 120cm (48in) long. Small fish, such as liquorice gouramis (*Parosphromenus deissneri*), are happier in small tanks about 30cm (12in) long.

The fish usually appreciate some floating plant cover, but make sure there are some caves and hidey-holes near the bottom as well. Some species will use these as spawning sites, and females that are being harassed by a male will find refuge in them.

Labyrinthfishes tend to be warmth-loving, so set the temperature at about 27°C (80°F) and use soft, acidic water. Not all species need soft water to breed, but it is a good idea to use it if you are unsure about the particular requirements of a species.

Place a pair in the aquarium and feed them well with live foods while they are in the tank. Most species will spawn within a few days, but this will depend upon what condition they were in before being introduced.

Male bubblenesters will set about building a nest as soon as they are comfortable. Initially, the female will find a quiet spot to observe his antics. Once the nest is completed to the male's satisfaction, he will display to the female and try to entice her into the nest. A ripe female will follow him back and spawning will take place. Both sexes help to collect the eggs and place them in the nest.

Once spawning is complete, remove the female. When the fry are free-swimming, take out the male as well. When breeding any mouthbrooders it is important to keep the male apart from females for at least two weeks after spawning so that you can feed him up again. Males can starve to death if they are bred too frequently.

Above: Use aquarium sealant to glue rocks together to form permanent caves and other structures. Do make sure that the sealant has cured for at least 48 hours before using any rock formations in the aquarium.

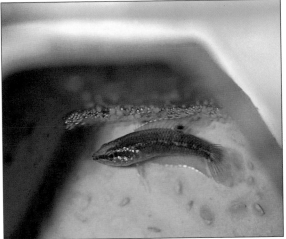

Above: This male Parosphromenus sumatranus *has built his bubblenest in a flower-pot laid on its side. To build it, he has had to make repeated trips to the surface to collect air to form each bubble.*

Left: *Male Siamese fighters are happy to build their bubblenests without any plants at all. This one, seen from directly above the water surface, has used some pieces of azolla in his.*

Mouthbrooding anabantoids are fairly unusual in the trade, but well worth seeking out if you are interested in breeding aquarium fish.

Place an adult pair in the breeding setup and feed them plenty of live foods. Once well-fed and adjusted to their new homes, most pairs spawn within a month or two. Maintain the water quality with weekly partial (25%) water changes.

Courtship usually starts about four hours after dawn (remember to turn on the lights in the fish room). The male will approach a ripe female first and if she is in breeding condition he will start to display and spread his beautiful finnage. During this display he almost encircles his mate and his tail frequently taps her on the nose. They then embrace in a typical anabantoid way and about five eggs fall towards the bottom. The female picks these up and blows them towards the male. He catches them in his mouth and stores them in his brood pouch. Other embraces follow until the female has run out of eggs.

Pairs stay together, usually in or next to a pot or small cave, for the 10 to 14 days it takes the eggs to hatch. Once they are free-swimming, the fry are released by the male. If they were well-fed during the incubation period, pairs will often spawn again straight away, but back-to-back spawnings such as this can starve the male to death, as he does not eat while he is looking after the eggs.

Breeding setup

Tank measuring 60x30x30cm (24x12x12in).

Provide floating plants such as Riccia.

Reasonably soft, acidic water (up to 120 ppm, pH 6.5). Temperature 24-27°C (75-80°F).

Provide some rocks to form caves.

Sex differences

Males have much longer and more pointed finnage. When fully mature, they turn a lovely chestnut colour with a blue dot in the middle of each scale. Females lack this gaudy colour and remain a more subdued mottled brown.

Rearing the fry

As soon as they are released by the male (usually over a period of several days), the young will swim to the surface and seek cover among floating plants. They will take newly hatched brineshrimp and microworms as first foods and will grow very quickly, reaching 2.5cm (1in) in only a month.

Below: *This mature male chestnut betta has recently released his batch of fry, so his throat pouch has shrunk to normal size. Chestnut bettas may not be as showy as many other labyrinths, but they have a quiet charm all of their own.*

Siamese fighters are some of the most beautiful freshwater fish and available in many different fin shapes and colours.

Once in the breeding setup, a well-conditioned male usually builds a bubblenest about 15cm (6in) away from the female. While constructing the nest, he regularly visits his potential mate and displays his wonderful finnage. When the nest is 7.5-10cm (3-4in) across and the female seems to be trying to follow the male back to his nest, you can gently release her. Most pairs will spawn almost immediately, but some females need courting for a little longer. A male often nips or butts the female at this time and could kill her if she is not ready to spawn.

Once spawning starts, the eggs sink through the water column and are collected up, first by the male and later by the female. These are placed in the nest and another embrace takes place. Once spawning has finished, the female swims away and hides. Remove her immediately. The male looks after eggs and newly hatched fry for five days until they are free-swimming. Remove him at this stage.

Sex differences

Females have a white pimple at the vent that males never show. Most males in the trade are the long-finned type and easy to distinguish from females, but wild-type, short-finned males are also imported. These will kill another male if they are placed in the same aquarium.

Left: *A male tending his bubblenest. He gathers the eggs into one small area, which looks milky white because of the eggs' colour. This species rarely uses plant matter in its nest.*

Right: *This female is well filled with eggs. When being courted, she will develop a vertical chevron pattern along her body, a clear indication of her willingness to spawn.*

Breeding setup

Hardness and pH not critical.

Float a well-conditioned female full of eggs in a small tank or jar.

Tank measuring 60x30x30cm (24x12x12in).

Temperature 24-27°C (75-80°F).

Rocks to form caves.

Rearing the fry

The fry are small and need infusoria for the first few days, but should be taking newly hatched brineshrimp by the end of the first week. Within eight weeks they will start to sex out and males must be separated into individual quarters. You can buy small plastic tanks for fighting fish that house several fish separately, but you will need a lot of these to cope with a brood of over 100 fish!

THICK-LIPPED GOURAMI • *Colisa labiosa*

Aquarists have been spawning thick-lipped gouramis for many years and they remain firm favourites. Providing both fish are well conditioned on live foods and the female is full of eggs, most pairs will spawn within a few days.

Typically, this species builds its bubblenest at the surface among floating plants, but some males prefer to spawn in a cave. Either way, the male will regularly court the female during this construction work and eventually she will follow him back to the nest and spawn. This follows the typical anabantoid embrace, with the eggs floating upwards, where the male gathers them together in one area. More bubbles are added at this point to increase the depth of the nest.

After many embraces, more than 500 eggs will have been produced. The female is then chased away and the male cares for his eggs and nest over the next few days. The eggs hatch in a day or two and are free-swimming by the fourth day. Remove the male at this stage to protect the fry.

Right: Males build a nest, either at the surface in plants, as here, or occasionally in a cave. In this case, males must collect air from the surface to build a nest.

Below: This pair is about to embrace. During the embrace the male will fold himself around his mate and they will then flip over so that the female is upside down. The eggs and sperm are released in this position.

Rearing the fry

Fry need infusoria as a first food, followed 7-10 days later by newly hatched brineshrimp. Other fry foods are also accepted. If the brood is a large one, you will either have to use several rearing tanks or cull the surplus fry. Trying to rear all the babies in a 60cm (24in) aquarium will lead to overcrowding and pollution, which will kill all the fry.

Breeding setup

Water hardness and pH are not critical, as this fish will adapt to a wide range of conditions.

Floating plants such as Riccia.

Tank measuring 60x30x30cm (24x12x12in).

Temperature 24-27°C (75-80°F).

Caves for females to hide in if harassed.

Sex differences

Males have much larger and more pointed dorsal and anal fins. They also have a beautiful blue throat and bold blue vertical stripes along their flanks. Females have less blue striping and are usually plumper.

LIQUORICE GOURAMI • *Parosphromenus deissneri*

Liquorice gouramis are a relatively recent addition to the fishkeeping hobby and an instant success with anyone who loves pretty little fish.

While they are in the breeding setup, feed the pair on brineshrimp and other small live foods. The male will take up residence in the plastic tube, while the female remains in the main part of the aquarium.

Courtship is initiated by the male and involves fin-flaring and swaying the body to and fro. If she is ready to breed, the female will follow him back to the tube and after a little more courting the pair will embrace. They produce about six eggs, which are collected up by the pair and stuck to the upper surface of the tube. After some more embraces, the female is chased out of the tube and the male starts to add bubbles to the nest. Remove the female at this stage. The eggs take 72 hours to hatch and the male can then be removed.

Rearing the fry

The fry take newly hatched brineshrimp as soon as they are free-swimming. They grow quickly and may need to be spread out into several tanks. Change at least 10% of the water weekly.

Sex differences

Males are slimmer and more brightly coloured than females. Sexing is not easy with fish that are immature or out of breeding condition.

Above: *A beautiful male in full breeding regalia. Sadly, this colour is only present shortly before spawning occurs or when the male is kept in perfect conditions.*

Below: *Ripe females are enticed under the nest by the male's splendid colours and display. Only use well conditioned females such as this one for breeding.*

Breeding setup

Keep the tank well clear of bright light.

Very soft, acidic water only 7.5cm (3in) deep. (Up to 50 ppm, pH below 6.)

Include a small plant as a hiding place for the female.

Tank measuring 30x15x15cm (12x6x6in). This species does really well in a small breeding tank.

Provide a plastic pipe 5cm (2in) in diameter floating in the water as a spawning site.

This huge group of fish contains in excess of 1,000 species worldwide. Nearly all are limited to freshwater environments and the ancestral species date back to before the continents started to break up. This means that the group as a whole has had a long time to develop many different breeding strategies. Some species, including the corydoras, are very easy to breed, while others are far more difficult and require very specific conditions before they will breed in captivity. Certain species have never bred outside their native homeland.

As well as the corydoras, other members of the Callichthyidae family are commonly bred in captivity. *Hoplosternum, Megalechis* and *Callichthys* build a bubblenest into which eggs are laid and then guarded by the male. In theory, *Dianema* does

Left: A typical habitat in the Amazon, home to many commonly kept catfish species. Aerial tree roots hanging down into the water and rotten trunks and branches provide refuges.

the same; it looks very similar to the other two species, yet it has proved almost impossible for aquarists to breed it with any regularity.

Apart from Callichthyidae, the Loricariidae are the most commonly bred catfish. Many species within this group practise brood care, with the male looking after the eggs and young until they are free-swimming. In some species, the male must be present at the birth to help the embryos break out of their eggshells. Without his intervention, the young would probably die within the egg.

Catfish have other interesting breeding strategies. Members of Hexanematichthys mouthbrood their young in a similar way to some cichlids. Even more bizarre is *Platystacus*. Females of this species push their eggs onto their abdomen, where they stick. As the eggs develop, stalks grow out from the mother until the eggs are wafting backwards and forwards in the water current.

Several catfish genera use internal fertilisation, just like livebearers. However, the eggs are released before they can develop into fully formed babies. Several *Synodontis* species are known to be the

Left: A female Corydoras paleatus resting on a flat rock in the aquarium. It is at this moment that sperm is sprayed from her vent over the eggs held in her pelvic fins.

cuckoos of the aquatic world. They dash between a pair of spawning mouthbrooding cichlids and scatter their milt and eggs among them. The female cichlid accidentally picks up the eggs and cares for them as if they were her own, mouthbrooding both her eggs and those of the catfish together. The catfish hatch out first and gobble up the cichlid fry as they hatch.

Typical spawning setup

With all catfish, it is best to use a long-term setup housing only the catfish you wish to breed, rather than a temporary setup just put together for the spawning. Include plenty of rockwork, bogwood, caves and plant life. Feed the adults well and be patient. Many species will breed eventually, but in a community aquarium the eggs or fry are lost, because the other fish eat them.

Filtration

The aquarium should include a bubble-up sponge filter to help maintain the water quality. Avoid filters that produce strong water currents at this stage, since small fry may be present that can be sucked into the filter unit. Since this is a long-term setup, it is important to include lighting to encourage plant growth. You can fit a suitable fluorescent tube into an aquarium hood to simulate daylight conditions.

Water changes

Regular partial water changes are also important. For most species, the water should be soft to neutral and slightly acidic. This will vary according to species, so check the conditions that prevail in their natural habitat. Water temperatures will also vary, but 25-28°C (77-82°F) will suit most species.

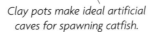
Clay pots make ideal artificial caves for spawning catfish.

Pieces of bogwood are essential to make many loricariids feel at home.

Left: *Male loricariids protect their eggs and newly hatched fry. Commonly, the male sits right over the top of the eggs to keep them hidden from possible predators.*

BRISTLENOSE CATFISH • *Ancistrus dolichopterus*

Bristlenose catfish appreciate a well-planted tank containing a good growth of algae. To encourage algae to form, try to position the aquarium where it will receive full sunlight for at least part of the day. Include good filtration and aeration. Feed the adults on a mixture of live, frozen and commercial dry foods, as well as vegetable matter.

Spawning is often triggered by a large water change, but most well-fed pairs will breed if they can find a suitable spawning site. During the breeding season (in winter), males become territorial, driving other males away. Females are more tolerant, accepting other fish in their 'domain', including females of their own species.

Pairs that are ready to spawn will adjourn to the male's nest site, where the female will lay at least 30 – but usually 50 or more – bright-orange eggs. Once fertilised, the male drives off his mate and takes care of the developing eggs by himself. These hatch five days later and after a further five days, the youngsters are ready to venture away from the safety of their father's nest. This is when, in a community tank, many fry are eaten.

Left: *This head shot shows the branched bristles of a fully mature male. Young males have much smaller bristles and fewer of them. Those on the cheeks are the last to develop.*

Sex differences

Females have smaller bristles that are hardly branched on their noses. Males tend to be larger in body size than females.

Rearing the fry

Initially, the male will try to supervise his offspring and keep them close by, but as they grow they become much bolder and soon venture well away from his protection. By this stage, the male will usually have found another mate (or the same one again) and may be looking after the next clutch of eggs. Youngsters eat all kinds of crushed vegetable matter, as well as any live foods that settle on the gravel. A good bloom of algae will encourage fry growth, as will newly hatched brineshrimp once they settle on the substrate.

Breeding setup

Water 24-27°C (75-80°F). Up to 150 ppm, pH 7.

Use a 60x30x30cm (24x12x12in) aquarium that has been permanently set up for breeding bristlenose catfish.

Cryptocoryne

Cabomba

Clay pots

Vallisneria

Algae growth

Bogwood with holes

This is an easy species to breed and regularly spawns in a community aquarium. Although individual pairs will breed, most breeders prefer to spawn the fish in groups of six or more.

Courtship is instigated by the male, who rubs his barbels across the female's back. Once she is sufficiently aroused, she will return his caresses and eventually mouth over his vent. At this stage, the female is sideways on to her mate and he will shudder into an S-shape as he releases sperm into her mouth. She then settles on the gravel for a few minutes, during which time the sperm travels through her gut to be expelled from her anus over a newly released batch of eggs. Four to six eggs are fertilised in this way each time and then pushed onto a suitable surface to develop. This is normally a broadleaved plant, but could be the front glass or a clump of plants. The eggs are 1.75mm (0.07in) in diameter and clear or opaque. They hatch in four days, but it will be another three days before the newborns are ready to feed.

Sex differences

Males have elongated fins (particularly dorsal and pectoral fins), although this characteristic had been lost to a certain extent in captive-bred strains. However, recent imports have re-established the trait. Females have very plump bodies when they are ready to spawn.

Rearing the fry

Newborn youngsters look like little tadpoles with their dorsal, caudal and anal fins joined up. They are large enough to manage microworms and brineshrimp as a first food, but will also accept powdered fry food once it has sunk to the substrate. The young grow rapidly and can reach 2.5cm (1in) in only eight weeks, by which time they will have their adult coloration and finnage.

Breeding setup

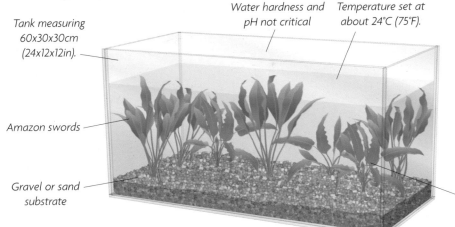

Tank measuring 60x30x30cm (24x12x12in).

Water hardness and pH not critical

Temperature set at about 24°C (75°F).

Amazon swords

Gravel or sand substrate

Cryptocoryne

Above: A group of peppered catfish (partially obscured by eggs) during the spawning frenzy. Surprisingly, the female probably returns to the same male to obtain sperm to fertilise each batch of eggs.

This is a very tolerant species that will spawn in a wide range of conditions, given a reasonably sized aquarium.

Males build a large bubblenest under a floating leaf or piece of polystyrene, breaking off from time to time to court a ripe female. When the nest is ready and the female has been sufficiently aroused, the pair will move under the nest and circle each other upside down. Eggs are deposited into the nest and, once spawning has finished, the female is chased away. Remove her from the tank at this point. The male will fiercely protect his nest until the eggs hatch in about three days. Remove him now and allow the fry to fend for themselves.

Rearing the fry

The fry become free-swimming on the fourth or fifth day and will eat newly hatched brineshrimp or microworms from then on. They will accept larger foods within a week and grow to 2.5cm (1in) in only a month. Being bottom-feeders, they do best when fed on sinking foods, such as grindalworms and whiteworms, but continue to offer them brineshrimp and other crustacean-based foods, as these contain essential elements of their diet. Tablet, granular and sinking pellets are also worth including. These fish will eat just about all the time and need good filtration in their aquarium to keep them healthy.

Breeding setup

Tank measuring 90x30x30cm (36x12x12in).

Large floating leaves such as water lilies or a piece of polystyrene floating on the surface.

Set the temperature at about 24°C (75°F).

Soft, slightly acidic water (75-100 ppm, pH 6.5).

Right: A female hoplo perches on a rock. This is typical behaviour for this species, which tends to spend more time swimming in midwater than many other catfish.

Sex differences

Females are much plumper than males and lack the thicker rays and long extensions to the first rays of the pectoral fins. Males may also show a bright blue-violet sheen on the ventral region.

UPSIDE-DOWN CATFISH • *Synodontis nigriventris*

House an individual pair in a well-planted 45cm (18in) aquarium and condition them on plenty of live foods. Since they may be seasonal spawners, it could be many months before they spawn.

Once settled into their new quarters, the pair will stake out a particular cave as their home. When they are in spawning condition, they dig a pit in the substrate and lay their eggs into it. Since the pit is normally dug under an overhang during the night, you may not realise straightaway that spawning has taken place. Both parents protect the nest and newly hatched young.

Sex differences

These fish can be difficult to sex until they are fully mature, when females are plumper and lighter in colour than males.

Right: The upside-down catfish not only rests upside down under a leaf or rock, but actually swims around in midwater in the same way, hence its common name.

Breeding setup

Set the temperature at 26°C (79°F).

Soft, slightly acidic water (75 ppm, pH 6.5).

Tank measuring 60x30x30cm (24x12x12in).

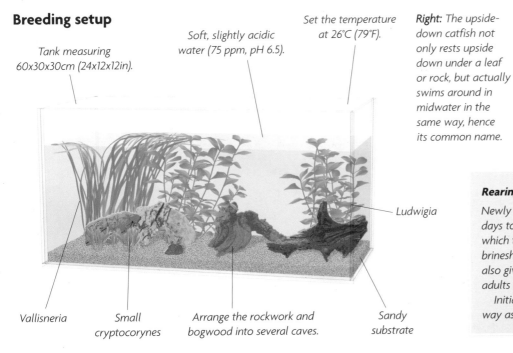

Ludwigia

Vallisneria

Small cryptocorynes

Arrange the rockwork and bogwood into several caves.

Sandy substrate

Rearing the fry

Newly hatched youngsters take four days to become free-swimming, after which they will feed on newly hatched brineshrimp and microworms. You can also give them powdered fry foods. The adults are best removed at this stage.

Initially, the fry swim in the same way as other fish, but by two months of age they will switch to the upside down mode for which they are famous. At this time they tend to congregate as a shoal and are found in large groups tucked away in caves during the day. They accept tubifex and grindalworms, as well as larger-sized, prepared growth foods and tablet foods.

Killifishes are distributed worldwide throughout most tropical freshwater systems and are highly adaptable. Many come from very soft acidic waters, others are found in some of the hardest water of any aquatic habitat, and some can be found in the most saline conditions (six times more saline than seawater!) Find an oasis in a desert and you will often find a unique species of killifish living in it.

These remarkable creatures have developed many different methods of reproduction to cope with whatever environmental problems they may have to deal with. In general, they can be divided into two main groups: fish that lay their eggs in plants and those that bury them in the substrate. The plant-spawners live in habitats where, although there may be seasonal variations in water levels, there will always be some water. The eggs of this group usually hatch in about two weeks.

Left: Killifish have adapted to a wide range of conditions. Their greatest challenge, though, are transitory pools like these. During the rainy season they are full of water and ideal habitats for fish.

Substrate-spawners

The substrate-spawners have developed because their habitats may dry up completely. Their eggs remain safely buried until the rains come, then the embryo breaks out and the life cycle starts all over again. Incubation periods will vary depending upon the species and conditions. The eggs of these species pass through several resting periods, during which their development is halted. These are called diapauses and most substrate-spawners pass through two of them before the embryo hatches. The reason

Above: Towards the end of the dry season, the pool has dried up and all the fish have died. Remarkably, killifish eggs buried in the substrate hatch out once the pool fills with water again.

for these resting periods is so that all the eggs do not hatch at the same time. The first downpour may be only sufficient to produce a few centimetres of water that soon dries out again. Any fry born at this time will die off.

Bear in mind that the demarcation between the two spawning groups is not always completely clear-cut. Some species will spawn either into the substrate or into plants, depending upon the prevailing conditions. Even certain strains of one species may breed in one way, while nearly all the others breed the other way.

With such a widespread and diverse range, it is not surprising to find that a number of fish have evolved different breeding strategies from the rest. Most aquarists are surprised to learn that some killifishes care for their eggs and young. The American flagfish (*Jordanella floridae*) is one of these. Males of this species dig a pit into which the female lays her eggs. These are protected by the male until they have hatched and the fry are free-swimming.

Another departure from the norm is internal fertilisation of the eggs. Several killifish genera have developed this breeding method. Some *Cynolebias* males have a modified anal fin that is used to transfer sperm to the female's vent. This is very similar to the behaviour of many livebearers; indeed, the dividing line between egglaying and livebearing killifishes can be very blurred.

Another unusual killifish is *Rivulus marmoratus*. This species has both male and female reproductive organs and is perfectly capable of fertilising its own

Left: A female American flagfish (Jordanella floridae). *She has a black spot in the dorsal fin and is fuller in the body.*

Below: A male American flagfish. *This species is unusual because males protect the eggs and young. During a week or more the adults will spawn into a nest and produce up to 70 eggs.*

place about 5cm (2in) of peat on the surface. After a week the peat will have become waterlogged and perfect for breeding. Keep a single male to two or three females in the breeding setup for about a week. Then move the fish and plants into another aquarium with fresh substrate, drain off the egg-laden substrate and place it in a plastic bag. Leave it for several weeks or even months, depending upon the species, before returning it to the water.

eggs – a very useful strategy if a single specimen finds itself in a new habitat. Many species of livebearer can store sperm so that a single pregnant female can start a whole new colony by herself. A single specimen of this killifish can do the same.

Typical breeding setup

Most killifish breeders tend to use small tanks measuring 30x20x20cm (12x8x8in) to house a single male and two or three females. Include a clump of Java moss or an artificial spawning mop, but little else. Eggs are laid almost daily; carefully pick them off the mop and place them in another small aquarium to hatch. If you are using a clump of Java moss, move it to a hatching tank every week, by which time it should hold a good number of eggs.

Substrate-spawners require a waterlogged peat substrate and a clump or two of Java moss for cover. To produce the peat layer, fill the aquarium with rainwater filtered through activated carbon and

Right: Spawning mops are *one of the essential pieces of equipment that anyone who wants to breed killifish will have to make. This one has a cork attached to it to keep it at the surface. See page 11 for guidance on making spawning mops.*

51

In the wild, there are many different colour morphs and subspecies of this species. Most are typical plant-spawners, but some prefer to spawn in the substrate; try to find out from the breeder or dealer which type you have.

Keeping one male to two or three females reduces the pressure on the females. Feed the adults plenty of small live foods while they are in the breeding tank. Courtship consists of the male fin-flaring and posturing in front of a female. If she is ready to spawn, the pair will move above the spawning mop and then dive into it side by side. They shudder into an S-shape as they expel eggs and milt. The eggs are clear and measure about 1.25mm (0.05in) in diameter.

It is a good idea to harvest the eggs every day during late afternoon or early evening. Since most eggs are laid early in the morning, this gives the shells time to harden off a little before you handle them. A single adult female may produce 10-20 eggs per day, but three to five is average. They take 10-12 days to hatch out.

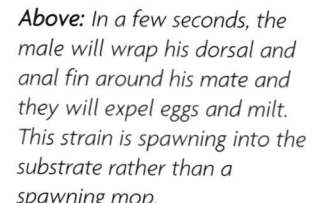

Above: *In a few seconds, the male will wrap his dorsal and anal fin around his mate and they will expel eggs and milt. This strain is spawning into the substrate rather than a spawning mop.*

Sex differences

Males are larger, much more brightly coloured and have points on the top and bottom of the caudal fin.

Rearing the fry

The fry start feeding almost as soon as they have hatched. Most youngsters are large enough to manage newly hatched brineshrimp straightaway, but infusoria and microworms also make good first foods. The young grow very rapidly and, provided they are not crowded, reach 5cm (2in) in two to three months. This species greedily accepts flake, frozen and live foods.

Breeding setup

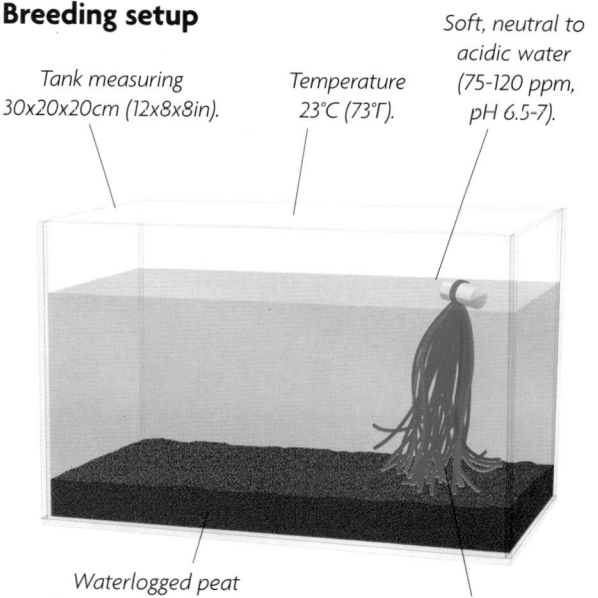

Tank measuring 30x20x20cm (12x8x8in).

Temperature 23°C (73°F).

Soft, neutral to acidic water (75-120 ppm, pH 6.5-7).

Waterlogged peat substrate as an alternative spawning medium.

Provide an artificial spawning mop.

SPARKLING PANCHAX • *Aplocheilus lineatus*

There are several different forms of this fish and if you are lucky enough to come across the golden form (sometimes called the golden wonder killi), it is well worth keeping.

Since this fish is not sensitive to pH and hardness, your normal tapwater (once treated with a water conditioner) will be suitable. Place a single male and two or three females in the tank and feed them well with a good-quality flake food and some live foods.

On most mornings, the male will court several different females until he finds one willing to spawn. Eggs are deposited near the surface among mop strands. Collect these and hatch them in a tank measuring 30x20x20cm (12x8x8in). They hatch after 14 days and will feed almost immediately.

Sex differences

Males have larger fins, brighter golden iridescent scales and paler black vertical stripes. In the golden form, they are a brilliant gold all over. Females tend to remain smaller.

Below: *This pair is courting near the bottom, but they usually lay their eggs near the water surface in plants or spawning mops. A large female will produce 10 to 20 eggs each day.*

Breeding setup

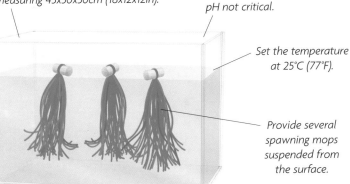

Tank measuring 45x30x30cm (18x12x12in).

Water hardness and pH not critical.

Set the temperature at 25°C (77°F).

Provide several spawning mops suspended from the surface.

Below: *Developing eggs stuck on a fine-leaved plant. They take 14 days to hatch, by which time you can see the babies' black eyes. Initially, just their tails will show, but they soon shake off the eggshell.*

Rearing the fry

The fry will take fine powdered fry foods and newly hatched brineshrimp. Since they mostly feed at the surface, it is a good idea to install a light above their tank so that the brineshrimp swim up to the surface. Keep the youngsters well fed and rear any significantly smaller fry separately, as they may be eaten by their larger siblings.

This beautiful killifish does well in hard water and will live happily in a normal community aquarium. It is very easy to breed and quite prolific, and makes a good starter fish for someone who has never bred a killifish before.

A group of one male to three or four females will produce the best results, although in a larger aquarium you could keep two males to six females. Courtship continues throughout the day, with a male flaring his fins and displaying to any female he can find. Most of these approaches are from the rear and side, rather than directly head-on. He will often nip or butt her in the ventral region at this time. If she is willing, they will move to the male's spawning mop. Here, the pair will dive into the mop (usually the same place each time) and release eggs and milt deep within the fronds.

Eggs tend to be laid in the tightest part of the mop, close to the knot. They are clear and 1.25mm (0.05in) in diameter. Collect them a few hours after spawning to allow the shells to harden, which will make them easier to handle. Hatch them in a 25x15x15cm (10x6x6in) tank, spread out over the bottom. They take up to 14 days to develop and the fry start to feed a day or two after hatching.

Above: A beautiful male Jamaican large-scaled killifish. In the wild, this species lives in shallow brackish water. Some areas of thick plant growth can be found in this habitat, but generally it is a mangrove swamp.

Rearing the fry

The fry are easy to rear on microworms and newly hatched brineshrimp. You can also offer them fry and growth foods.

Sex differences

The male's enlarged dorsal and anal fins are a beautiful golden colour. The body is also suffused with gold, overlaid with a blue sheen. Females have clear fins and a black stripe running the full length of the body.

Breeding setup

Set the temperature at 23°C (73°F).

Tank measuring 45x25x25cm (18x10x10in).

Hard, slight;y alkaline water with a minimum hardness of 150 ppm and a pH of 7.8.

Provide several spawning mops.

BEIRA NOTHO • *Nothobranchius melanospilus*

Every aquarist interested in breeding fish should try their hand at spawning one of the substrate-spawning killis, and this genus contains some of the easiest. It is remarkable to see hundreds of baby fish suddenly appear in a tank where just a few hours ago there was only peat and water.

Place a single male to two or three females in the breeding setup for about a week. Courtship takes place just about every morning, with at least one female actually mating. During courtship, the male flares his fins and tries to manoeuvre his potential mate so that he is parallel to her. As they dive into the peat, both his dorsal and anal fins will wrap around her body. Trembling side by side, they produce eggs and milt before breaking apart and swimming away.

After a week, transfer the adults into another aquarium and remove the peat using a fine-meshed net. Place the peat in a plastic bag and keep it at 23°C (73°F) for six weeks. Then spread it out over the bottom of an empty aquarium and refill with rainwater filtered through carbon. A few hours later you will see the fry swimming about in the aquarium.

Above: *The pair dive into the peat substrate, usually throwing a cloud of peat into the water. By the time this has settled, the pair will have finished their embrace and be exiting the substrate.*

Breeding setup

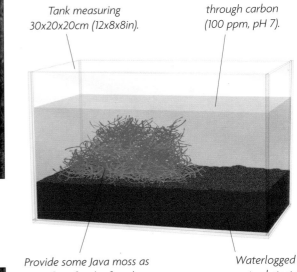

Tank measuring 30x20x20cm (12x8x8in).

Use rainwater filtered through carbon (100 ppm, pH 7).

Provide some Java moss as a refuge for the female.

Waterlogged peat substrate.

Sex differences

Males have the most beautiful coloration and larger fins. Females are smaller and generally a drab grey colour.

Right: *During mating, the male wraps his dorsal and anal fins around the female. Most spawnings take place deep in the peat substrate and by this stage, the eggs and milt have been released.*

Rearing the fry

Feed the fry on newly hatched brineshrimp and microworms. As soon as they are large enough, transfer them to a new aquarium filled with neutral, moderately soft water. Re-dry the peat for a further 14 days and then make it wet again. This usually produces a few more youngsters.

RAINBOWFISHES

Rainbowfishes have a great deal going for them in terms of ease of keeping, compatibility with other fish and absolutely stunning colours. Sadly, they are often overlooked by beginners, because as young fish they are usually rather drab-looking and often high-priced. The reason for the higher price is that nearly all rainbowfishes sold in the trade are captive-bred by small-scale breeders and tend to take longer to reach saleable size.

Breeding most species is fairly easy, since they fall neatly into two main categories: those that produce large numbers of small eggs and those that produce small numbers of large eggs. The advantage of those in the first category is that one spawning may number several hundred offspring. The disadvantage is that the fry require infusoria for several weeks before they can take newly hatched brineshrimp. Powdered fry foods can also be fed initially, but you must take great care that neither infusoria nor powdered fry foods are allowed to pollute the water; rainbowfishes are very susceptible to ammonia poisoning or a reduction in the oxygen content of the water. For this reason, include gentle aeration in fry tanks and add a small bubble-up sponge filter when the fry are a week old.

The species that produce smaller numbers of large eggs are much easier to deal with, as the fry are large enough to take brineshrimp straightaway. They also tend to grow more quickly, and although they do not produce such large numbers of eggs all at once,

Left: *Male threadfin rainbowfish (Iriatherina werneri) are beautiful when they display. This species lays large numbers of small eggs and their fry require infusoria as a first food.*

Below: *This beautiful river on the Guatemalan/ Mexican border is tinted blue by the high level of dissolved salts in the water. This river is home to a species of rainbowfish in the genus* Chirostoma.

Left: *Red New Guinea rainbowfish (Glossolepis incisus) grow to over 13cm (5in) in body length, yet still produce small eggs and fry. Feed the fry on infusoria as a first food.*

most will lay a few each day, every day. They are also unlikely to eat their eggs and in some cases can be flock-bred in a well-planted aquarium.

As a general guide the following genera produce small eggs: Chilatherina, Glossolepis, Iriatherina, Melanotaenia and Rhadinocentrus. All of these will need infusoria as a first food.

What is interesting about this list is that the adult size of the fish has very little to do with what size eggs it produces. Many of the smaller species, such as *Pseudomugil*, produce large eggs.

Many mature male rainbowfish develop a hump behind the head. This adult male Chilatherina bleheri *clearly displays this characteristic.*

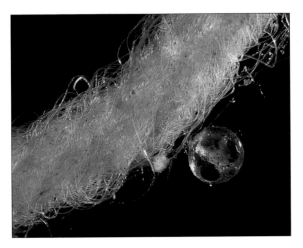

Above: *A developing egg of Bleher's rainbowfish. The eggs are clear when first laid, but as the embryo develops, the black eyes can be seen through the shell. Unfertilised eggs will turn white and be affected by fungus.*

Right: *Bleher's rainbowfish (*Chilatherina bleheri*) becomes sexually mature at about 5cm (2in), but will actually grow to 13cm (5in) in captivity. The male, shown here, exhibits brighter colour and more elongated fins than the female.*

Typical spawning setup

Despite the differences between rainbowfishes, most can be bred in much the same way. The aquarium size will vary depending on the size of the species to be bred, but an average aquarium would be 60x30x30cm (24x12x12in) for fish up to 7.5cm (3in) long, rising to a 120x30x30cm (48x12x12in) for fish measuring 10cm (4in) or more.

Suspend spawning mops from the surface and spread a few around the bottom of the tank. No substrate is necessary, but gentle aeration is important. Water quality should be hard and moderately alkaline for most species, although a few do better in softer, neutral water.

Place a mature group of two males and four females in the breeding tank and leave them together for a week. Feed them regularly with live and frozen foods as well as a good-quality flake food. Most groups spawn shortly after first light and while not all females will breed every day, several will spawn during the course of a week.

Check the mops for eggs and then remove the adults. The eggs can be left in situ until they hatch; rear the fry on infusoria or brineshrimp as needed.

An alternative to this system is one where the adults are permanently set up and you move the egg-filled mops over to a hatching and rearing tank. If the eggs are large ones, pick them off carefully and spread them out over the aquarium bottom to hatch. This ensures better water movement around the egg, which means that more oxygen is present and a higher percentage of eggs will hatch. This method is not practical with those species that produce small eggs, but gentle aeration near the mops helps.

NEON RAINBOWFISH • *Melanotaenia praecox*

This is one of the more recent introductions and has to be one of the most beautiful rainbowfish ever discovered. It is a small fish that only grows to about 5cm (2in). A shoal of two males and four females can produce over 100 eggs per week.

Courtship takes place every morning, shortly after first light. Both males will chase the females around until they find one willing to spawn. They dive down into the top of the Java moss and scatter a batch of eggs into the plant. Further couplings take place, both with the original female and possibly others, depending on who is ready to spawn. The eggs take a week or so to hatch. It is possible to 'colony breed' this species in a well-planted aquarium, but for best results, remove the Java moss to another tank for hatching and rearing.

Right: It will be a few more months before this pair of young neon rainbowfish is ready to spawn, but the male (above) already shows a slightly deeper body than his mate. Plenty of live foods in their diet will improve their coloration.

Breeding setup

Tank measuring 60x30x30cm (24x12x12in).

Include a bubble-up sponge filter.

Water 100 ppm plus, pH 7.5 plus. Set the temperature at 24-26°C (75-79°F).

Place a large clump of Java moss on the bottom.

Rearing the fry

The fry need infusoria or a very fine powdered fry food for a week before they can manage newly hatched brineshrimp and microworms. However, microworms are not a particularly good food for rainbowfishes because they fall to the bottom and most rainbowfish fry stay very close to the surface.

Sex differences

Neon rainbowfish can be sexed very early, as males develop a very deep body shape, a characteristic not normally seen in other rainbowfishes until they are old. Males also have more colour in their fins. The tip of the first dorsal fin extends beyond the origin of the second.

Sadly, these superb community fish are not seen as often as they should be. They are easy to breed, beautifully coloured and relatively hardy. They are not fussy with regard to hardness or pH and seem to do well in a very wide range of water conditions.

Use two males and a group of six females for breeding. The males will set up their own territories, with one taking possession of a spawning mop at each end of the tank. The females tend to stay in the middle of the aquarium. Every morning the males will display for the females; fins are flared and their colour is heightened. Apart from the odd skirmish, males tend to ignore each other and concentrate their efforts on the females. Eventually, a female will follow a male back to his mop to spawn. When this happens, the fish swim to the mop from the lower reaches of the aquarium and then upwards next to each other. Near the top they push their bodies together and into the mop, releasing eggs and milt.

Most success has been achieved when the eggs are picked off the mop and spread out in another aquarium to hatch, which takes 14 days.

Breeding setup

Tank measuring 60x30x30cm (24x12x12in).

Suspend several spawning mops at each end.

Water 100 ppm and pH 7.5 plus.

Set the temperature at 24°C (75°F).

Sex differences

Males have bright yellow tips to all their fins. They also have larger fins than females and the first dorsal fin tip extends beyond the origin of the second. This is a very useful method of sexing most rainbowfishes.

Left: This is a mature male in ideal breeding condition. As males grow older, they often develop a pigeon chest, by which time most fish are too old to breed from. The ideal age for breeding stock is about eight months old.

Cichlids are a fascinating group of fish to breed because, as far as we know, all species practise brood care of some sort. They are usually divided into two main groups: mouthbrooders and substrate-spawners. However, things are nowhere near as clear-cut as this, since these two main categories can be subdivided depending on who cares for the young, what substrate is used to lay their eggs on and who guards the territory.

Mouthbrooding cichlids
Mouthbrooders pick up their fertilised eggs and hold them in the mouth until the young are large enough to venture out into the world. Some species will take their babies back into the mouth in times of danger, while others ignore them once they have been released. The big advantage these fish have over most other fish is that their eggs are relatively safe in the adult's mouth and most will at least reach the free-swimming stage. The downside is that fewer eggs are produced in each spawning and most adults stop feeding while brooding their eggs. This means they need longer to recover between spawnings than many of their substrate-spawning cousins.

The most commonly seen mouthbrooders are mbuna from Lake Malawi. In these species, the female cares for the eggs and males will spawn with any passing ripe female. Mixed communities of these

Right: Mouthbrooders like this Oreochromis mossambicus *often care for their young long after they have initially released them. Whenever danger threatens, they will take all the babies back into the mouth for protection.*

fish often produce hybrids, so if you want to breed mbuna, keep them in a species-only aquarium with one male to three or four females.

Substrate-spawning cichlids
We tend to think of substrate-spawners as fish that lay their eggs on a rock or in a pit in the gravel. However, in the case of cichlids, the substrate means any surface to which the fish attaches its eggs – a leaf, the roof of a cave, a vertical piece of slate or even the aquarium glass.

Once laid, one or both parents will care for the eggs, regularly fanning them to keep well-oxygenated water passing over them, removing any eggs that show signs of fungus and chasing away any fish that approaches. Some species have to help their fry out of the egg case when they hatch, otherwise the young will die trapped inside.

In most cichlids, the female undertakes the bulk of caring for the youngsters, while the male takes a more active role in defending the territory. In some species this has reached the point where a male will

guard a territory that includes several brooding females, a strategy known as harem polygyny.

Once the eggs have hatched, most substrate-spawners move their offspring into a pit dug in the gravel. When they are free-swimming, the youngsters are herded about towards the best feeding sites. Care usually continues until the adults are ready to breed again, at which time they will often return to the same spawning site they used before. A few species will breed with their older brood still in tow and the older babies may even take an active part in caring for their younger siblings.

Some substrate-spawners spawn right out in the open on a rock or in a pit. They are described as open-brooders and tend to be large fish with less to fear from predators. Cave-brooders are often smaller, more timid fish that appreciate plenty of places to hide.

Typical spawning setup
Since most community fish will attempt to eat the eggs or young of any fish that breed in the tank, it is always best to set up a separate breeding tank. This applies particularly to cichlids, since they often dig up plants, attack other fish and generally cause mayhem in a community aquarium when breeding.

The spawning setup should be large enough to accommodate comfortably both parents or a breeding group of adults. For large species, you might need an aquarium 1.8m (6ft) long. Since it will be a permanent home for the adults, it should include filtration (an external power filter is probably best) and suitable decor. For most species this means plenty of rockwork, caves and other hideaways. Dwarf cichlids will appreciate

some plant cover, while angelfish and discus use large Amazon swordplants as spawning sites.

As you might expect from such a diverse group, water conditions are going to vary according to where each species lives in the wild. Many cichlids require hard alkaline water (particularly those from Malawi, Tanganyika and Central America), while others need soft acidic water. Almost the whole of the *Apistogramma* genus falls into this group. For this reason, check where each species comes from and try to recreate the natural water and temperature conditions for your fish.

Many open breeders, particularly rams, prefer to spawn on a substrate of flat pebbles.

A male jewel cichlid (Hemichromis bimaculatus) moves in to fertilise the eggs after they have been laid by the female.

Broadleaved plants, such as this Amazon sword, make ideal spawning substrates for angelfish and discus.

61

RAINBOW CICHLID • *Herotilapia multispinosa*

Rainbow cichlids are relatively peaceful and can be kept with fish of a similar size (10cm/4in). They will start breeding when they are about 7.5cm (3in).

Place a mature pair in the aquarium by themselves and feed them on a mixture of frozen, live, flake and pellet foods, plus some vegetable matter. After some days or weeks, you will notice the pair cleaning the surface of a stone with their mouths. At this time, they will be showing a darker ventral area with almost jet black pelvic and anal fins. Once they are happy with the spawning site, the female will pass over the stone and lay a row of eggs. The male follows afterwards and fertilises them. When all the eggs are laid, he moves away to concentrate on guarding the territory, while his mate fans and cares for the eggs. On the third day after spawning, the female often moves the eggs to a pit and at this time you can see the almost invisible tails thrashing about. The fry become free-swimming on the seventh day.

Sex differences

Males tend to be larger than females and have longer, more pointed dorsal and anal fins.

Breeding setup

Water conditions 100 ppm plus, pH 7 plus. Temperature 24-27°C (75-80°F).

Planted areas using tough species, such as Amazon swords. (Soft-leaved plants are likely to be eaten.)

Tank measuring 60x30x30cm (24x12x12in).

Use a bubble-up sponge filter.

Regularly change 25% of the water.

Plenty of large flat stones scattered about the bottom.

Gravel substrate

Left: An adult pair. Although the female (the lower fish) is not very full of roe, they would certainly be worth setting up in a breeding tank.

Rearing the fry

The adults continue to care for their fry until they are ready to spawn again. Feed the young on small live foods and commercial fry foods.

In many aquarium shops, this fish will still be found under its old name of *Pseudotropheus zebra*. It is an aggressive species, normally kept in a mixed mbuna community aquarium. Due to the risk of hybridisation, do not save any fry produced in this sort of setup. For breeding purposes, house a single male and four or more females in a separate breeding tank. The adults will eat all types of food, but some vegetable matter is important in their diet.

The male is polygamous and will spawn with any ripe female. The female takes the eggs into her mouth and broods them until the fry are free-swimming. She continues to care for them for a further week or so after they leave her mouth.

It is best to remove a brooding female carefully into a separate aquarium before she releases her fry. Do this by gently netting her and then using a bowl to lift both mother and net across to the maternity aquarium. This way she will remain in water and be less likely to spit out her eggs. Once the fry are released, the female can be returned to the breeding tank.

Sex differences

Males have large, well-defined eggspots on their anal fin. In females, these are much fainter or not present. There are several different colour forms.

Above: *This mature male* Metriaclima zebra *has many eggspots in his anal fin. These encourage the female to mouth this area and pick up sperm to fertilise her eggs.*

Breeding setup

Minimum size aquarium 90x30x30cm (36x12x12in).

Hard, alkaline water (200 ppm, pH 8.3)

Temperature set at 26°C (79°F).

Provide good filtration and aeration.

Plenty of rockwork built up into a wall-like structure.

Rearing the fry

Youngsters will eat newly hatched brineshrimp and microworms from the start, but feed them some growth foods as well.

MAGARAE SHELL-DWELLER • *Neolamprologus calliurus*

This beautiful shell-dweller was originally imported under the name of *Lamprologus* sp. 'Magarae' because it was collected in the Magarae area of Burundi.

When the breeding tank is ready, add a group of one male and four females. They will soon set about digging away the gravel underneath each shell and burying them in positions they are happy with. The females take up residence in a shell just big enough to accommodate them, while the male guards his harem. Courtship is started by a ripe female, who approaches the male and tries to entice him back to her shell. He flares his fins at her and together the pair return to her shell. The eggs are laid inside the shell and the mother allows the youngsters to live alongside her until they are four or five weeks old. They are then banished to live under other shells or between rocks in other parts of the aquarium. Initially, both parents look after the young.

Sex differences

Males are very distinctive, because unlike all other shell-dwellers, they have a lyre-shaped caudal fin. They also have long extensions on their anal and pelvic fins, as well as being almost twice the size of their mates.

Breeding setup

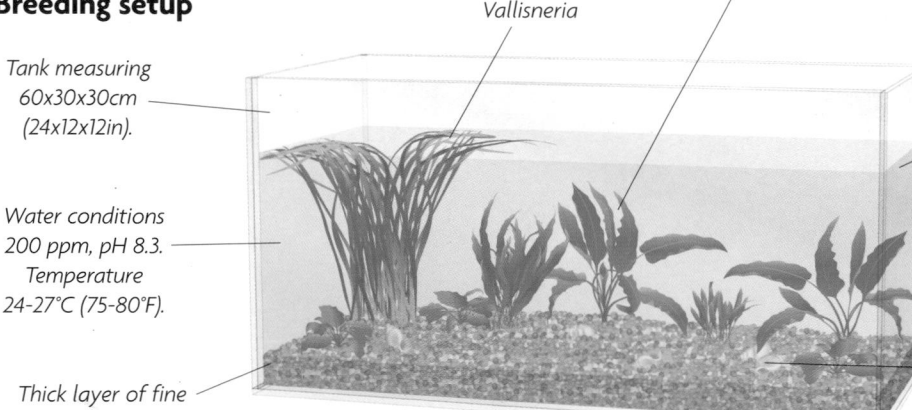

Tank measuring 60x30x30cm (24x12x12in).

Water conditions 200 ppm, pH 8.3. Temperature 24-27°C (75-80°F).

Thick layer of fine gravel over the bottom.

Vallisneria

Cryptocoryne

Use an external power filter. Position the intake at least 15cm (6in) above the aquarium bottom and direct the return across the surface.

Various-sized snail shells scattered across the substrate.

Above: *A fully mature male Magarae shell-dweller. Adults like this clearly exhibit the fin extension, not present on immature males or females.*

Rearing the fry

Feeding the fry while they are living with the female is fairly easy if you have a meat baster! Use it to squirt newly hatched brineshrimp towards the shell mouth, where both mother and youngsters will happily eat them.

Rams are one of the most popular cichlids kept in captivity. They are readily available and fit in well in a community aquarium. Despite their small size (just 5cm/2in), they are open brooders. When selecting potential breeders, look at all the fish in the shop and watch how they move around. Fish that have already paired off will try to stay close to each other all the time and may even have staked out a territory. Choose the best-looking pair or buy six youngsters to grow up.

If the adults are well fed on live foods, most pairs will spawn within a month of being placed in the breeding tank. When both fish are ready to breed, they usually select and clean a flattish stone before the female lays a row of about 200 eggs on it. Some pairs prefer to hide from view and spawn in a cave. Once two fish have paired off, remove the rest to separate quarters.

During courtship, both fish spread their fins wide and show enhanced colours. The eggs take three days to hatch, but are not free-swimming until the seventh day.

Sex differences

Males are larger, have a longer second ray in the dorsal fin and their anal fin is more pointed. They are also less plump than females, but all these differences are only clearly visible on fully mature fish.

Breeding setup

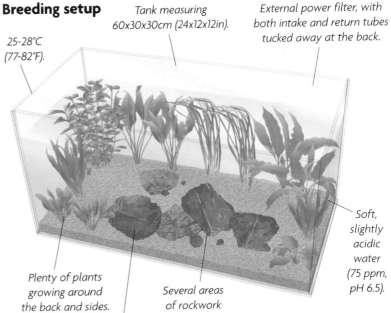

Tank measuring 60x30x30cm (24x12x12in).

External power filter, with both intake and return tubes tucked away at the back.

25-28°C (77-82°F).

Soft, slightly acidic water (75 ppm, pH 6.5).

Plenty of plants growing around the back and sides.

Several areas of rockwork

At least one flattish stone placed right out in the open.

Left: *A pair of fish guarding their eggs. The male is the upper fish and is staring threateningly at the camera.*

Rearing the fry

Compared with most cichlid fry, these young are small, but most broods can tackle microworms as a first food and can manage brineshrimp in three days. After a few weeks, the fry will be moving well away from their parents, ready for life by themselves.

For many aquarists, kribensis was not only their first cichlid to breed, but also their first egglayer and a typical cave-spawner. It is best to grow on six or more youngsters together and allow them to pair off naturally. Alternatively, buy a mature pair. Most fish seem willing to accept a mature mate, providing it is in breeding condition. While not so often seen these days, it is still one of the most beautiful dwarf cichlids in the hobby.

When a pair have settled into their surroundings, the female will select a suitable spawning cave and entice her mate into it. Here they usually spawn on the roof, laying up to 250 eggs. These take three days to hatch and the fry become free-swimming on the seventh day.

Sex differences

Males have a golden crescent in the top half of the tail, which also has elongated rays in the central portion. The dorsal and anal fins are pointed. Females are smaller and tend to be plumper.

Above: *A mature male. When in spawning condition, he develops a great deal more colour and a clear red patch on his stomach. Well-marked males have spots in both the dorsal and upper caudal fin.*

Breeding setup

Some areas of plant growth.

Tank measuring 60x30x30cm (24x12x12in).

Moderately soft, neutral water (100 ppm, pH 7).

Include plenty of rockwork and caves for the pair to choose as breeding sites.

Set temperature at 25-27°C (77-80°F).

Right: *Females like to keep their recently hatched brood close to them. When young like these are fed on newly hatched brineshrimp, they have a bright orange belly for a few hours afterwards.*

Rearing the fry

Adults will rear their brood without any problems. Feed the fry brineshrimp and microworms at first, and add some fry and growth foods to the diet later on as they grow. Remove the babies when their parents drive them away from the old nesting site and prepare to spawn again.

Before all the mouthbrooding Lake Malawi cichlids were introduced to the hobby, this was the mouthbrooder to keep. Its popularity has waned somewhat now, but if this is your first attempt at breeding mouthbrooding cichlids, it is a good one to choose. It is not fussy about water conditions and eats all foods.

Place a mature, ripe female and a male in the aquarium. Spawning usually takes place in a pit dug in some out-of-the-way corner. Courtship can be a little rough, with females almost dragged to the spawning pit. Eventually, the pair will swim in circles nose to tail, expelling eggs and milt as they go. Once these have been fertilised, the female picks them up in her mouth. When spawning is complete she swims off and finds a quiet hideaway. Now that the male's job is done, remove him from the tank. The female will incubate the eggs for two weeks before releasing free-swimming fry.

Above: A female with a mouthful of recently hatched young just visible underneath her mouth. Whenever she thinks her babies are threatened, she will take them back into her mouth.

Sex differences

Males tend to be larger and are more colourful, particularly when they are in breeding condition.

Breeding setup

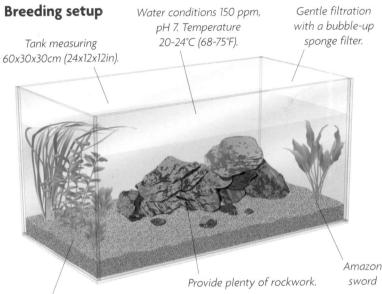

Tank measuring 60x30x30cm (24x12x12in).

Water conditions 150 ppm, pH 7. Temperature 20-24°C (68-75°F).

Gentle filtration with a bubble-up sponge filter.

Provide plenty of rockwork.

Amazon sword

Some plant cover, such as these vallisneria, ludwigia and cryptocoryne.

Left: This well-conditioned pair of dwarf Egyptian mouthbrooders is ideal for breeding from. They used to be a staple of the aquarium hobby, but may be difficult to find in the trade now.

Rearing the fry

For the first week the fry are taken back into their mother's mouth at night and whenever danger threatens. Feed them on newly hatched brineshrimp and powdered fry foods. Remove the female after a week and rear up the fry by themselves. Providing they are well fed and have enough space, they grow very quickly. Youngsters half the adult size will breed successfully.

ANGELFISH • *Pterophyllum scalare*

Angelfish are one of the best-known of all aquarium fish; even non-fishkeepers recognise them! If you house an adult pair by themselves in a well-planted aquarium, there is a good chance that they will breed and rear their brood in the natural way.

During courtship, both fish will flash their fins at each other and often engage in 'kissing'. In fact, this is a test of strength and, providing neither has a clear advantage over the other, they will usually decide that they are a compatible pair.

Spawning takes place during the early evening after the pair have cleaned the spawning site, such as a stone or piece of slate. The female lays her eggs in rows and they are fertilised by the male. To rear them artificially, remove the stone with the eggs at this stage and place them in an aquarium with a fine stream of air bubbles passing close to them. Add one drop per litre of 5% methylene blue as a fungicide. The eggs hatch in three days and are free-swimming on the eighth day.

Rearing the fry

Fry accept newly hatched brineshrimp or microworms as a first food and grow quickly. They are soon able to take commercial growth food.

Right: *This pair of silver angels are similar to wild-caught angelfish. Wild-caught fish tend to be deeper in the body and have longer fins than their captive-bred cousins.*

Below: *Angelfish use any vertical surface as a substrate. Here, they are laying their eggs on a piece of slate. The darker, upper fish is the male of this couple.*

Sex differences

Sexing young angelfish can be a real problem, but once they are sexually mature, it becomes fairly easy if you know what you are looking for. With the fish facing directly towards you, look at the area just behind its pelvic fins. If this bulges out, it is a female. You can make a final check when the fish are in spawning condition, because the male's genital papilla is pointed.

Breeding setup

Tank measuring 60x30x45cm (24x12x18in).

Water conditions for wild-caught fishes 50 ppm, pH below 6.5.

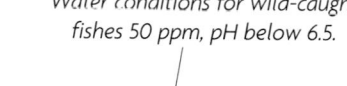

Pieces of slate propped up against the back glass.

Set the temperature at 25-28°C (77-82°F).

DISCUS • *Symphysodon sp.*

Discus are often thought of as a great challenge to breed, when in fact they do not present too many problems provided you give them the correct conditions and food. Rear up a group of six youngsters in a permanently set up aquarium and feed them on a wide range of foods, including frozen bloodworm, brineshrimp, etc. Commercial discus foods are also available now.

As they approach sexual maturity, your school of discus will start to separate out into pairs and stake out a territory. Leave the best pair in the permanent setup and move the others into another aquarium out of the way.

Spawning usually takes place on a flat vertical surface, but many pairs choose to lay their eggs on a broad plant leaf. The eggs are fanned for three days before they hatch and the fry become free-swimming on the seventh day.

Sex differences

The only certain way of sexing discus is to wait until they are sexually mature and in breeding condition. At this time, the ovipositor will clearly protrude and in females it is blunt and larger than in males.

Right: This pair of discus is rearing a brood of fry. At this stage in their development, the babies are totally dependent on their parents for food. Later they will eat newly hatched brineshrimp.

Rearing the fry

Discus feed their fry on mucus secreted from the sides of their bodies. As soon as the babies are free-swimming, they move to their parents' sides and start feeding, but after ten days they travel further afield to look for other foods. You can now feed them on newly hatched brineshrimp. The young can be separated from their parents at a month old.

Breeding setup

Very soft, slightly acidic water (up to 75 ppm, pH 6.5).

Provide some pieces of slate or an upturned clay pot.

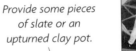

Tank measuring 120x30x45cm (48x12x18in).

Water temperature 28°C (82°F).

Change 25% of the water weekly.

Plenty of natural plants, particularly Amazon swords.

Large external canister filter. Position the return pipe close to the surface to provide gentle movement but not a strong water current.

There are hundreds of popular fish that do not fall into the main groups of aquarium fish, but are still commonly kept and bred by aquarists. Many have unusual or interesting breeding habits.

Many species of fish in several different areas around the world fertilise their eggs internally. Ricefish *(Oryzias)*, which are closely related to the killifish, fertilise their eggs internally and then expel them as a clump that hangs below the female's vent for a few hours. The female then finds a suitable cluster of fine-leaved plants onto which she can brush the eggs. *Xenopoecilus* do something similar, except that in their natural habitat there are few suitable spawning sites, so the female carries the clump around with her until the young start to hatch ten days later.

The butterflyfish *(Pantodon buchholzi)* from Africa is another species that has started down the path to livebearing. The male's anal fin has been modified into a copulatory organ, with which he fertilises the female internally. Once mating has occurred she swims off and expels the eggs later.

Freshwater gobies

Gobies have found great popularity within the marine hobby, but there are also a few wonderful freshwater fish within the group that are offered through the trade. There are literally thousands of species worldwide and many of these practise brood care in one form or another. Many species produce thousands of extremely small fry that have proved almost impossible to rear in captivity, but a few species breed easily and produce large, robust fry.

Left: Ricefish (Oryzias melastigmus) are halfway to becoming livebearers. If they held on to their eggs for a few more weeks before releasing them, most aquarists would think of them as livebearers, because by that stage the fry would be free-swimming, exactly like guppy fry.

Below: Butterflyfishes (Pantodon buchholzi) need plenty of live foods if they are to breed. In the wild, they feed on flies and mosquitoes falling on the water surface. In captivity, condition them on fruitflies and mosquito larvae.

Pipefish

Another really odd-looking fish with an interesting method of reproduction is the pipefish. Many are marine species, but a few venture into brackish water and some live in freshwater. Males have two ridges along the ventral surface that form a V-shaped groove. During mating the female deposits her eggs into this groove, where they develop until the young are

Above: *Many species of goby can be bred in captivity.* Chlamydogobius eremius *hails from Australian deserts and is one of the best for beginners to try their hand at breeding.*

Left: *A clutch of* Chlamydogobius eremius *eggs. These have been tucked away under a stone. The fish will also use small caves and tubes to spawn in.*

free-swimming. In some species, the groove closes over to form a pouch in which the eggs develop just as they do in seahorses. In these species, the fry are born fully formed and ready to fend for themselves.

Snakeheads

Snakeheads are another fascinating group of fish. These large predators can learn to recognise their owner and become tame enough to feed by hand. They are close cousins of the anabantoids and although they do not build a bubblenest, their spawning behaviour is similar. Some species clear away plants from their chosen spawning site and lay eggs that float up to the surface. The male guards the eggs until they hatch and may continue brood care for several weeks afterwards. These species tend to live in still-water environments. A number of other species are mouthbrooders in which the male looks after the eggs and young for nearly two weeks. These live in flowing waters and produce much smaller broods of young.

Typical spawning setup

Given such a wide variety of species, it is impossible to define a typical spawning setup. As a general guide, it is important to find out as much

as possible about the native habitat of any fish you wish to breed and reproduce those conditions in your aquarium as closely as you can.

Even in this very limited introduction to species that do not fit in one of the main aquarium fish categories, you can see that their methods of reproduction vary considerably – and there are probably many more reproduction methods yet to be discovered. The most startling discovery of recent times was probably not the fact that the coelacanth was still alive after science had written it off as being extinct some 65 million years ago, but that this ancient species is a livebearing fish.

Clumps of plants in the breeding tank help to define territories and reduce aggression between rival males.

CEYLONESE GREEN SNAKEHEAD • *Channa gachua*

Even though it is a predator that grows to about 25cm (10in) in length, the beautiful, mouthbrooding snakehead makes a wonderful pet fish.

Since sexing juveniles is impossible, place six fish in the breeding setup and allow them to grow up together. Once a compatible pair have sexed out, they will start picking on the other fish. Initially, only the weakest fish will be nipped and chased by the pair, while the others are left alone. Once the weakest is removed, the pair then start on the next weakest until only two fish are left. These will be a pair (up until this point it is almost impossible to be sure) and can be left in the aquarium until they spawn. Make sure you feed the pair with plenty of live foods, such as earthworms and pieces of fish, to help bring them into breeding condition.

Being a secretive species, courtship usually passes unnoticed, but we do know that the fish embrace in the same way as labyrinthfishes and that their eggs float up to the water surface. The male then gathers them up in his mouth and keeps them in a throat pouch until the fry are free-swimming. Once the fry have been released, remove the male to another aquarium.

Breeding setup

Tank measuring 90x30x30cm (36x12x12in).

Set the temperature at 27°C (80°F).

Moderately soft, neutral water (100 ppm, pH 7).

Plenty of plants, rockwork and large flowerpots to create hiding places.

Rearing the fry

Not surprisingly, the fry will eat brineshrimp as soon as they are free-swimming. Larger live foods can be added later, but make sure you also offer some dead foods, such as whitebait or shrimps. Small, slow-growing fry will be eaten by their larger siblings.

Sex differences

In common with most snakeheads, this species is very difficult to sex. Females tend to be a little plumper than males, but this may not be a reliable guide if the male has recently eaten a large meal!

Right: *A Ceylonese green snakehead in typical pose – looking for food! Its eyes are positioned high up and are forward pointing so the fish has binocular vision – essential for judging distance and catching prey.*

Desert gobies are a really hardy variety that fit in well with a community aquarium. Being bottom-dwellers, they fill an area of the tank that can look a little bare at times.

When they breed, the male makes one of the pots the centre of his territory, while the female tends to hide among the plants or lives in another pot, well clear of the male. If well fed with live and frozen foods, most pairs will spawn every few weeks.

Spawning takes place in the male's pot and the eggs are laid on one of the pot walls. After spawning, remove the female and leave the male to guard his eggs. These take about six days to hatch and become free-swimming, at which time the male should be removed. Once the fry start to sex out move them to larger quarters. The original pair can now be moved back in to spawn again or you can use a succession of spawning tanks and move the breeding pair from one to another as they produce new broods.

Sex differences

Females are a drab mottled brown with almost clear fins, but males have bright yellow bodies and blue fins edged in white.

Rearing the fry

The fry eat newly hatched brineshrimp or microworms as first foods. Provide powdered fry foods, followed by granular growth foods as well. The fry sex out at about four months and males will want to establish territories. They will harm each other in a small, overcrowded aquarium, particularly if there are not enough hiding places.

Below: The desert goby is a pretty fish, well worth hunting for in aquarium shops. When he is in breeding colour, this male will show more of the beautiful yellow for which this species is renowned.

Breeding setup

Tank measuring 60x30x30cm (24x12x12in).

Set the temperature at 26°C (79°F).

Include gentle filtration.

This hardwater species needs a hardness in excess of 200 ppm and a pH of 7.5-8.0.

Litter the bottom of the tank with plenty of overturned pots.

Provide an area of plant cover.

Sand or gravel substrate.

When peacock gobies were first introduced to the aquarium hobby they commanded a high price and were very much sought after. Many years on, they are still much admired, although the price has come down to more reasonable levels.

To breed peacock gobies, place a single pair in the breeding setup and feed them on plenty of small live foods. Include gentle filtration (a bubble-up sponge filter is best for this) and change 10% of the water each week. The male will lay claim to a suitable spawning area, while the female finds a quiet corner away from him.

Once the fish are in breeding condition, the male will start courting the female whenever he sees her. Eventually, he entices her back to his spawning cave, where they clean the spawning site. This is usually a rock face tucked away in an almost inaccessible spot. Once the female has laid her eggs, the male chases her away, so remove her from the tank. The male guards the eggs and fry for four to six days after they have hatched. By then they are free-swimming and searching for food. Remove the male at this stage.

Sex differences

Males develop a distinct hump on the forehead and tend to grow larger. The female has smaller finnage and a more rounded belly, which turns bright yellow when she is in breeding condition.

Rearing the fry

The young are large enough to tackle brineshrimp as a first food, and grow rapidly. Feed them some powdered fry food as well as live foods so that they become used to taking both. They take several months to sex out, by which time the male's hump is visible.

Breeding setup

Tank measuring 45x30x30cm (18x12x12in).

Hard, neutral water (150 ppm, pH 7). Temperature 24°C (75°F).

Plenty of rockwork or bogwood. Position the decor to create several caves and hidey-holes.

Gravel or sand substrate.

Provide some plant cover.

Above: *A pair courting prior to spawning. By this stage, most pairs will be ready to start laying eggs within a few minutes. Once it has started, egglaying may take anything up to one hour to complete.*

Above: *For such a small goby, the eggs are very large. Initially they are clear (like these) but soon you can see the embryos' eyes developing. The male will sit on his clutch of eggs and protect them from allcomers.*

This is one of the real oddballs of the aquarium world. It is a recent introduction that has gained favour with those aquarists who like a fish that is a little different but that will still do well in a normal aquarium. The adults are not fussy about food and will eat a good-quality flake food, as well as any live or frozen foods they are offered.

The male's colours change dramatically when he is courting a ripe female. He develops a beautiful golden hue, with black appearing right across his back. His fins go black as well.

During mating, the male wraps his anal and dorsal fins around the female. This usually takes place just after first light and a few hours later the female expels fertilised eggs. These hang by a thread from her vent for the 16 or so days it takes for them to develop. Shortly before they are due to hatch, most clusters fall off. Since the adults eat any fry they find, it is important to move any females carrying eggs to a heavily planted maternity aquarium. As soon as she is free of the eggs, she can be returned to the main colony tank.

Left: A female Celebes buntingi with developing eggs. The white egg close to her body and near the front of the clump is infertile. The rest of the eggs are healthy and well developed; even the embryos' eyes are visible.

Sex differences

Males have elongated dorsal and anal fins. Females have enlarged pelvic fins.

Breeding setup

Tank measuring 60x30x30cm (24x12x12in).

Set the temperature at 23-26°C (73-79°F).

The water should be soft to slightly hard and slightly acidic. (up to 100 ppm/pH 6.5).

Include filtration and carry out regular partial water changes.

Provide plenty of plants towards the back and sides.

Rearing the fry

The fry will take newly hatched brineshrimp as soon as they are properly free-swimming. Offer them fry and growth foods as well. They take about three months to sex out, at which point the pelvic fins of females start to lengthen. Males develop their longer finnage about four weeks later.

INDEX

Page numbers in **bold** indicate major entries; *italics* refer to captions and annotations; plain type indicates other text entries.

CREDITS

Practical photographs by Geoffrey Rogers © Interpet Publishing.

The publishers would like to thank the following photographers for providing images, credited here by page number and position: B(Bottom), T(Top), C(Centre), BL(Bottom Left), etc.

Aqua Press (M-P & C Piednoir): Title page, copyright page, 14(B), 17, 18(BL, BC), 20, 22(C, BC), 23, 24(BL, BR), 27(T, B), 28(T, B), 35, 38, 41(C), 42(T), 51(TL, C), 53(BL, BC), 56(T, BC), 58, 63, 66(TR), 68(T), 69, 79(BR), 71(TL), 74(T, B)
John Feltwell (Garden Matters): 25(R)
Ad Konings, Cichlid Press: 64
Derek Lambert: 34, 36, 40, 44(T), 54, 56(CR), 75
Arend van den Nieuwenhuizen: 14(T), 16, 19(T), 24(TR), 31(TC, TR), 32(TC), 37, 41(BC), 42(T), 43(T), 44(B), 46, 47, 48, 49, 52, 55(T, B), 66(B), 70(T), 72, 73
Photomax (Max Gibbs): 6, 21, 26, 29, 30(TC, CR), 33(TL, BL), 39(B), 59, 60, 61(BL), 62, 65, 67(T, B), 68(B)
Ian Sainthouse: 50
Mike Sandford: 45(B), 57(T,B)
W A Tomey: 32(BR), 71(BL)
K A Webb: 39(TR)

Illustrations by Phil Holmes and Stuart Watkinson
© Interpet Publishing.

The publishers would like to thank Mary Bailey and Heaver Tropics, Ash, Kent, for their help during the preparation of this book.

The information and recommendations in this book are given without any guarantees on the part of the author and publisher, who disclaim any liability with the use of this material.